The Duchess of Malfi by John Webster

John Webster is known primarily for his two Jacobean tragedies, The Duchess of Malfi and The White Devil. Much of the detail and chronology of his life that led to these two pivotal works is, however, unknown.

His father, a carriage maker also named John Webster, married a blacksmith's daughter, Elizabeth Coates, on November 4th, 1577, and it is likely that Webster was born within a year or two in or near London.

The family lived in St. Sepulchre's parish. Both his father and his uncle, Edward Webster, were Freemen of the Merchant Taylors' Company and Webster attended Merchant Taylors' School in Suffolk Lane, London.

Some accounts say he began to study law but nothing is certain although there are some legal aspects to his later works to suggest this may have been so.

By 1602, Webster was employed working as part of various teams of playwrights on history plays, though unfortunately most were never printed and therefore do not survive. These include a tragedy Caesar's Fall (written with Michael Drayton, Thomas Dekker, Thomas Middleton and Anthony Munday), and a collaboration with Thomas Dekker; Christmas Comes but Once a Year (1602). This factory line assembly of plays may seem rather odd to us today but plays then ran for much shorter durations and consequently a steady supply had to be assured.

Webster's relationship with Dekker seems to have been a good one. Together they wrote Sir Thomas Wyatt, printed in 1607, although it is thought first performed in 1602 and two city comedies, Westward Ho! in 1604 and Northward Ho! in 1605. It seems Webster also adapted, in 1604, John Marston's The Malcontent for staging by the King's Men.

On March 18th, 1606 Webster married the 17-year-old Sara Peniall at St Mary's Church, Islington. Sara was 7 months pregnant and marrying during Lent required the issuing of a special permit, hence the certainty of the date. Their first child, John, was baptised at the parish of St Dunstan-in-the-West on March 8th, 1606. Records show that on the death of a neighbour, who died in 1617, several bequests were made to the Webster family and it is therefore thought that other children were born to the couple.

Despite his ability to write comedy, and to collaborate with others, Webster is remembered best for his sole authorship on two brooding English tragedies based on Italian sources. The White Devil, retells the intrigues involving Vittoria Accoramboni, an Italian woman assassinated at the age of 28. It was performed at the open-air Red Bull Theatre in 1612 but was unsuccessful, perhaps being too high brow for a working-class audience.

In 1614 The Duchess of Malfi was first performed by the King's Men, most probably in the indoor Blackfriars Theatre and to a more high-brow audience. It proved to be more successful.

The play Guise, based on French history, was also written but him but no text has survived.

Webster wrote one more play on his own: The Devil's Law Case (c. 1617–1619), a tragicomedy.

He continued to write thereafter but always in collaboration and usually city comedies; Anything for a Quiet Life (c. 1621), with Thomas Middleton, and A Cure for a Cuckold (c. 1624), with William Rowley.

In 1624, he also co-wrote a topical play about a recent scandal, Keep the Widow Waking (with John Ford, Rowley and Dekker). The play itself is lost, although its plot is known from a court case.

There is also some certainty that he contributed to the tragicomedy The Fair Maid of the Inn with John Fletcher, John Ford, and Phillip Massinger. His Appius and Virginia, was probably written with Thomas Heywood, and is of uncertain date.

It is believed, mainly from Thomas Heywood's Hierarchie of the Blessed Angels (licensed 7 November 1634) that speaks of him in the past tense that John Webster had died at some point in that year of 1634.

Index of Contents
INTRODUCTORY NOTE
THE DUCHESS OF MALFI
DRAMATIS PERSONAE
ACT I
SCENE I
SCENE II
SCENE III
ACT II
SCENE I
SCENE II
SCENE III
SCENE IV
SCENE V
ACT III
SCENE I
SCENE II
SCENE III
SCENE IV
SCENE V
ACT IV
SCENE I
SCENE II
ACT V
SCENE I
SCENE II
SCENE III
SCENE IV

SCENE V

INTRODUCTORY NOTE

"The Duchess of Malfi" is based on a story in Painter's "Palace of Pleasure," translated from the Italian novelist, Bandello; and it is entirely possible that it has a foundation in fact. In any case, it portrays with a terrible vividness one side of the court life of the Italian Renaissance; and its picture of the fierce quest of pleasure, the recklessness of crime, and the worldliness of the great princes of the Church finds only too ready corroboration in the annals of the time.

Webster's tragedies come toward the close of the great series of tragedies of blood and revenge, in which "The Spanish Tragedy" and "Hamlet" are landmarks, but before decadence can fairly be said to have set in. He, indeed, loads his scene with horrors almost past the point which modern taste can bear; but the intensity of his dramatic situations, and his superb power of flashing in a single line a light into the recesses of the human heart at the crises of supreme emotion, redeems him from mere sensationalism, and places his best things in the first rank of dramatic writing.

THE DUCHESS OF MALFI

Dramatis Personae

FERDINAND [Duke of Calabria].
CARDINAL [his brother].
ANTONIO BOLOGNA, Steward of the Household to the Duchess].
DELIO [his friend].
DANIEL DE BOSOLA [Gentleman of the Horse to the Duchess].
CASTRUCCIO, an old Lord.
MARQUIS OF PESCARA.
COUNT MALATESTI.
RODERIGO,   }
SILVIO,   } Lords.
GRISOLAN,   }
DOCTOR.
The Several Madmen.

DUCHESS OF MALFI.
CARIOLA, her woman.
JULIA, Castruccio's wife, and the Cardinal's mistress.
Old Lady.

Ladies, Three Young Children, Two Pilgrims, Executioners, Court Officers, and Attendants.

ACT I

SCENE I [1]

[Enter **ANTONIO** and **DELIO**]

DELIO
You are welcome to your country, dear Antonio;
You have been long in France, and you return
A very formal Frenchman in your habit:
How do you like the French court?

ANTONIO
I admire it:
In seeking to reduce both state and people
To a fix'd order, their judicious king
Begins at home; quits first his royal palace
Of flattering sycophants, of dissolute
And infamous persons,—which he sweetly terms
His master's master-piece, the work of heaven;
Considering duly that a prince's court
Is like a common fountain, whence should flow
Pure silver drops in general, but if 't chance
Some curs'd example poison 't near the head,
Death and diseases through the whole land spread.
And what is 't makes this blessed government
But a most provident council, who dare freely
Inform him the corruption of the times?
Though some o' the court hold it presumption
To instruct princes what they ought to do,
It is a noble duty to inform them
What they ought to foresee.[2]—Here comes Bosola,
The only court-gall; yet I observe his railing
Is not for simple love of piety:
Indeed, he rails at those things which he wants;
Would be as lecherous, covetous, or proud,
Bloody, or envious, as any man,
If he had means to be so.—Here's the cardinal.

[Enter **CARDINAL** and **BOSOLA**]

BOSOLA
I do haunt you still.

CARDINAL.
So.

BOSOLA

I have done you better service than to be slighted thus. Miserable age, where only the reward of doing well is the doing of it!

CARDINAL.
You enforce your merit too much.

BOSOLA
I fell into the galleys in your service: where, for two years together, I wore two towels instead of a shirt, with a knot on the shoulder, after the fashion of a Roman mantle. Slighted thus! I will thrive some way. Black-birds fatten best in hard weather; why not I in these dog-days?

CARDINAL.
Would you could become honest!

BOSOLA
With all your divinity do but direct me the way to it. I have known many travel far for it, and yet return as arrant knaves as they went forth, because they carried themselves always along with them.

[Exit **CARDINAL**.]

Are you gone? Some fellows, they say, are possessed with the devil, but this great fellow were able to possess the greatest devil, and make him worse.

ANTONIO
He hath denied thee some suit?

BOSOLA
He and his brother are like plum-trees that grow crooked over standing-pools; they are rich and o'erladen with fruit, but none but crows, pies, and caterpillars feed on them. Could I be one of their flattering panders, I would hang on their ears like a horseleech, till I were full, and then drop off. I pray, leave me.
Who would rely upon these miserable dependencies, in expectation to be advanc'd to-morrow? What creature ever fed worse than hoping Tantalus? Nor ever died any man more fearfully than he that hoped for a pardon. There are rewards for hawks and dogs when they have done us service; but for a soldier that hazards his limbs in a battle, nothing but a kind of geometry is his last supportation.

DELIO
Geometry?

BOSOLA
Ay, to hang in a fair pair of slings, take his latter swing in the world upon an honourable pair of crutches, from hospital to hospital. Fare ye well, sir: and yet do not you scorn us; for places in the court are but like beds in the hospital, where this man's head lies at that man's foot, and so lower and lower.

[Exit.]

DELIO
I knew this fellow seven years in the galleys

For a notorious murder; and 'twas thought
The cardinal suborn'd it: he was releas'd
By the French general, Gaston de Foix,
When he recover'd Naples.

ANTONIO
'Tis great pity
He should be thus neglected: I have heard
He's very valiant. This foul melancholy
Will poison all his goodness; for, I'll tell you,
If too immoderate sleep be truly said
To be an inward rust unto the soul,
If then doth follow want of action
Breeds all black malcontents; and their close rearing,
Like moths in cloth, do hurt for want of wearing.

SCENE II[3]

ANTONIO, DELIO, [Enter **SILVIO, CASTRUCCIO, JULIA, RODERIGO** and **GRISOLAN**]

DELIO
The presence 'gins to fill: you promis'd me
To make me the partaker of the natures
Of some of your great courtiers.

ANTONIO
The lord cardinal's
And other strangers' that are now in court?
I shall.—Here comes the great Calabrian duke.

[Enter **FERDINAND** and **ATTENDANTS**]

FERDINAND
Who took the ring oftenest? [4]

SILVIO
Antonio Bologna, my lord.

FERDINAND
Our sister duchess' great-master of her household?
Give him the jewel.—
When shall we leave this sportive action, and fall to action indeed?

CASTRUCCIO
Methinks, my lord, you should not desire to go to war
in person.

FERDINAND
Now for some gravity.—Why, my lord?

CASTRUCCIO
It is fitting a soldier arise to be a prince, but not necessary a prince descend to be a captain.

FERDINAND
No?

CASTRUCCIO
No, my lord; he were far better do it by a deputy.

FERDINAND
Why should he not as well sleep or eat by a deputy?
This might take idle, offensive, and base office from him,
Whereas the other deprives him of honour.

CASTRUCCIO
Believe my experience, that realm is never long in quiet where the ruler is a soldier.

FERDINAND
Thou toldest me thy wife could not endure fighting.

CASTRUCCIO
True, my lord.

FERDINAND
And of a jest she broke of[5] a captain she met full of wounds: I have forgot it.

CASTRUCCIO
She told him, my lord, he was a pitiful fellow, to lie, like the children of Ismael, all in tents.[6]

FERDINAND
Why, there's a wit were able to undo all the chirurgeons[7] o' the city; for although gallants should quarrel, and had drawn their weapons, and were ready to go to it, yet her persuasions would make them put up.

CASTRUCCIO
That she would, my lord.—How do you like my Spanish gennet?[8]

RODERIGO.
He is all fire.

FERDINAND
I am of Pliny's opinion, I think he was begot by the wind; he runs as if he were ballass'd[9] with quicksilver.

SILVIO
True, my lord, he reels from the tilt often.

RODERIGO, GRISOLAN.
Ha, ha, ha!

FERDINAND
Why do you laugh? Methinks you that are courtiers should be my touch-wood, take fire when I give fire; that is, laugh when I laugh, were the subject never so witty.

CASTRUCCIO
True, my lord: I myself have heard a very good jest, and have scorn'd to seem to have so silly a wit as to understand it.

FERDINAND
But I can laugh at your fool, my lord.

CASTRUCCIO
He cannot speak, you know, but he makes faces; my lady cannot abide him.

FERDINAND
No?

CASTRUCCIO
Nor endure to be in merry company; for she says too much laughing, and too much company, fills her too full of the wrinkle.

FERDINAND
I would, then, have a mathematical instrument made for her face, that she might not laugh out of compass.—I shall shortly visit you at Milan, Lord Silvio.

SILVIO
Your grace shall arrive most welcome.

FERDINAND
You are a good horseman, Antonio; you have excellent riders in France: what do you think of good horsemanship?

ANTONIO
Nobly, my lord: as out of the Grecian horse issued many famous princes, so out of brave horsemanship arise the first sparks of growing resolution, that raise the mind to noble action.

FERDINAND
You have bespoke it worthily.

SILVIO
Your brother, the lord cardinal, and sister duchess.

[Enter **CARDINAL**, with **DUCHESS**, and **CARIOLA**]

CARDINAL
Are the galleys come about?

GRISOLAN
They are, my lord.

FERDINAND
Here 's the Lord Silvio is come to take his leave.

DELIO
Now, sir, your promise: what 's that cardinal?
I mean his temper? They say he 's a brave fellow,
Will play his five thousand crowns at tennis, dance,
Court ladies, and one that hath fought single combats.

ANTONIO
Some such flashes superficially hang on him for form; but observe his inward character: he is a melancholy churchman. The spring in his face is nothing but the engend'ring of toads; where he is jealous of any man, he lays worse plots for them than ever was impos'd on Hercules, for he strews in his way flatterers, panders, intelligencers, atheists, and a thousand such political monsters. He should have been Pope; but instead of coming to it by the primitive decency of the church, he did bestow bribes so largely and so impudently as if he would have carried it away without heaven's knowledge. Some good he hath done—

DELIO
You have given too much of him. What 's his brother?

ANTONIO
The duke there? A most perverse and turbulent nature.
What appears in him mirth is merely outside;
If he laught heartily, it is to laugh
All honesty out of fashion.

DELIO
Twins?

ANTONIO
In quality.
He speaks with others' tongues, and hears men's suits
With others' ears; will seem to sleep o' the bench
Only to entrap offenders in their answers;
Dooms men to death by information;
Rewards by hearsay.

DELIO
Then the law to him

Is like a foul, black cobweb to a spider,—
He makes it his dwelling and a prison
To entangle those shall feed him.

ANTONIO
Most true:
He never pays debts unless they be shrewd turns,
And those he will confess that he doth owe.
Last, for this brother there, the cardinal,
They that do flatter him most say oracles
Hang at his lips; and verily I believe them,
For the devil speaks in them.
But for their sister, the right noble duchess,
You never fix'd your eye on three fair medals
Cast in one figure, of so different temper.
For her discourse, it is so full of rapture,
You only will begin then to be sorry
When she doth end her speech, and wish, in wonder,
She held it less vain-glory to talk much,
Than your penance to hear her. Whilst she speaks,
She throws upon a man so sweet a look
That it were able to raise one to a galliard.[10]
That lay in a dead palsy, and to dote
On that sweet countenance; but in that look
There speaketh so divine a continence
As cuts off all lascivious and vain hope.
Her days are practis'd in such noble virtue,
That sure her nights, nay, more, her very sleeps,
Are more in heaven than other ladies' shrifts.
Let all sweet ladies break their flatt'ring glasses,
And dress themselves in her.

DELIO
Fie, Antonio,
You play the wire-drawer with her commendations.

ANTONIO
I 'll case the picture up: only thus much;
All her particular worth grows to this sum,—
She stains[11] the time past, lights the time to come.

CARIOLA
You must attend my lady in the gallery,
Some half and hour hence.

ANTONIO
I shall.

[Exeunt **ANTONIO** and **DELIO**]

FERDINAND
Sister, I have a suit to you.

DUCHESS
To me, sir?

FERDINAND
A gentleman here, Daniel de Bosola,
One that was in the galleys—

DUCHESS
Yes, I know him.

FERDINAND
A worthy fellow he is: pray, let me entreat for
The provisorship of your horse.

DUCHESS
Your knowledge of him
Commends him and prefers him.

FERDINAND
Call him hither.

[Exit **ATTENDANT**.]

We are now upon[12] parting. Good Lord Silvio,
Do us commend to all our noble friends
At the leaguer.

SILVIO
Sir, I shall.

DUCHESS
You are for Milan?

SILVIO
I am.

DUCHESS
Bring the caroches.[13]—We 'll bring you down
To the haven.

[Exeunt **DUCHESS, SILVIO, CASTRUCCIO, RODERIGO, GRISOLAN, CARIOLA, JULIA,** and **Attendants**.]

CARDINAL

Be sure you entertain that Bosola
For your intelligence.[14] I would not be seen in 't;
And therefore many times I have slighted him
When he did court our furtherance, as this morning.

FERDINAND
Antonio, the great-master of her household,
Had been far fitter.

CARDINAL
You are deceiv'd in him.
His nature is too honest for such business.—
He comes: I 'll leave you.

[Exit.]

[Re-enter **BOSOLA**]

BOSOLA
I was lur'd to you.

FERDINAND
My brother, here, the cardinal, could never
Abide you.

BOSOLA
Never since he was in my debt.

FERDINAND
May be some oblique character in your face
Made him suspect you.

BOSOLA
Doth he study physiognomy?
There 's no more credit to be given to the face
Than to a sick man's urine, which some call
The physician's whore, because she cozens[15] him.
He did suspect me wrongfully.

FERDINAND
For that
You must give great men leave to take their times.
Distrust doth cause us seldom be deceiv'd.
You see the oft shaking of the cedar-tree
Fastens it more at root.

BOSOLA
Yet take heed;

For to suspect a friend unworthily
Instructs him the next way to suspect you,
And prompts him to deceive you.

FERDINAND
There 's gold.

BOSOLA
So:
What follows? [Aside.] Never rain'd such showers as these
Without thunderbolts i' the tail of them.—Whose throat must I cut?

FERDINAND
Your inclination to shed blood rides post
Before my occasion to use you. I give you that
To live i' the court here, and observe the duchess;
To note all the particulars of her haviour,
What suitors do solicit her for marriage,
And whom she best affects. She 's a young widow:
I would not have her marry again.

BOSOLA
No, sir?

FERDINAND
Do not you ask the reason; but be satisfied.
I say I would not.

BOSOLA
It seems you would create me
One of your familiars.

FERDINAND
Familiar! What 's that?

BOSOLA
Why, a very quaint invisible devil in flesh,—
An intelligencer.[16]

FERDINAND
Such a kind of thriving thing
I would wish thee; and ere long thou mayst arrive
At a higher place by 't.

BOSOLA
Take your devils,
Which hell calls angels! These curs'd gifts would make
You a corrupter, me an impudent traitor;

And should I take these, they'd take me to hell.

FERDINAND
Sir, I'll take nothing from you that I have given.
There is a place that I procur'd for you
This morning, the provisorship o' the horse;
Have you heard on 't?

BOSOLA
No.

FERDINAND
'Tis yours: is 't not worth thanks?

BOSOLA
I would have you curse yourself now, that your bounty
(Which makes men truly noble) e'er should make me
A villain. O, that to avoid ingratitude
For the good deed you have done me, I must do
All the ill man can invent! Thus the devil
Candies all sins o'er; and what heaven terms vile,
That names he complimental.

FERDINAND
Be yourself;
Keep your old garb of melancholy; 'twill express
You envy those that stand above your reach,
Yet strive not to come near 'em. This will gain
Access to private lodgings, where yourself
May, like a politic dormouse—

BOSOLA
As I have seen some
Feed in a lord's dish, half asleep, not seeming
To listen to any talk; and yet these rogues
Have cut his throat in a dream. What's my place?
The provisorship o' the horse? Say, then, my corruption
Grew out of horse-dung: I am your creature.

FERDINAND
Away!

[Exit.]

BOSOLA
Let good men, for good deeds, covet good fame,
Since place and riches oft are bribes of shame.
Sometimes the devil doth preach.

[Exit.]

SCENE III [17]

[Enter **FERDINAND**, **DUCHESS**, **CARDINAL**, and **CARIOLA**]

CARDINAL
We are to part from you; and your own discretion
Must now be your director.

FERDINAND
You are a widow:
You know already what man is; and therefore
Let not youth, high promotion, eloquence—

CARDINAL
No,
Nor anything without the addition, honour,
Sway your high blood.

FERDINAND
Marry! they are most luxurious[18]
Will wed twice.

CARDINAL
O, fie!

FERDINAND
Their livers are more spotted
Than Laban's sheep.[19]

DUCHESS
Diamonds are of most value,
They say, that have pass'd through most jewellers' hands.

FERDINAND
Whores by that rule are precious.

DUCHESS
Will you hear me?
I 'll never marry.

CARDINAL
So most widows say;
But commonly that motion lasts no longer

Than the turning of an hour-glass: the funeral sermon
And it end both together.

FERDINAND
Now hear me:
You live in a rank pasture, here, i' the court;
There is a kind of honey-dew that 's deadly;
'T will poison your fame; look to 't. Be not cunning;
For they whose faces do belie their hearts
Are witches ere they arrive at twenty years,
Ay, and give the devil suck.

DUCHESS
This is terrible good counsel.

FERDINAND
Hypocrisy is woven of a fine small thread,
Subtler than Vulcan's engine:[20] yet, believe 't,
Your darkest actions, nay, your privat'st thoughts,
Will come to light.

CARDINAL
You may flatter yourself,
And take your own choice; privately be married
Under the eaves of night—

FERDINAND
Think 't the best voyage
That e'er you made; like the irregular crab,
Which, though 't goes backward, thinks that it goes right
Because it goes its own way: but observe,
Such weddings may more properly be said
To be executed than celebrated.

CARDINAL
The marriage night
Is the entrance into some prison.

FERDINAND
And those joys,
Those lustful pleasures, are like heavy sleeps
Which do fore-run man's mischief.

CARDINAL
Fare you well.
Wisdom begins at the end: remember it.

[Exit.]

DUCHESS
I think this speech between you both was studied,
It came so roundly off.

FERDINAND
You are my sister;
This was my father's poniard, do you see?
I 'd be loth to see 't look rusty, 'cause 'twas his.
I would have you give o'er these chargeable revels:
A visor and a mask are whispering-rooms
That were never built for goodness,—fare ye well—
And women like variety of courtship.
What cannot a neat knave with a smooth tale
Make a woman believe? Farewell, lusty widow.

[Exit.]

DUCHESS
Shall this move me? If all my royal kindred
Lay in my way unto this marriage,
I 'd make them my low footsteps. And even now,
Even in this hate, as men in some great battles,
By apprehending danger, have achiev'd
Almost impossible actions (I have heard soldiers say so),
So I through frights and threatenings will assay
This dangerous venture. Let old wives report
I wink'd and chose a husband.—Cariola,
To thy known secrecy I have given up
More than my life,—my fame.

CARIOLA
Both shall be safe;
For I 'll conceal this secret from the world
As warily as those that trade in poison
Keep poison from their children.

DUCHESS
Thy protestation
Is ingenious and hearty; I believe it.
Is Antonio come?

CARIOLA
He attends you.

DUCHESS
Good dear soul,
Leave me; but place thyself behind the arras,

Where thou mayst overhear us. Wish me good speed;
For I am going into a wilderness,
Where I shall find nor path nor friendly clue
To be my guide.

[**CARIOLA** goes behind the arras.]

[Enter **ANTONIO**]

I sent for you: sit down;
Take pen and ink, and write: are you ready?

ANTONIO
Yes.

DUCHESS
What did I say?

ANTONIO
That I should write somewhat.

DUCHESS
O, I remember.
After these triumphs and this large expense
It 's fit, like thrifty husbands,[21] we inquire
What 's laid up for to-morrow.

ANTONIO
So please your beauteous excellence.

DUCHESS
Beauteous!
Indeed, I thank you. I look young for your sake;
You have ta'en my cares upon you.

ANTONIO
I 'll fetch your grace
The particulars of your revenue and expense.

DUCHESS
O, you are
An upright treasurer: but you mistook;
For when I said I meant to make inquiry
What 's laid up for to-morrow, I did mean
What 's laid up yonder for me.

ANTONIO
Where?

DUCHESS
In heaven.
I am making my will (as 'tis fit princes should,
In perfect memory), and, I pray, sir, tell me,
Were not one better make it smiling, thus,
Than in deep groans and terrible ghastly looks,
As if the gifts we parted with procur'd[22]
That violent distraction?

ANTONIO
O, much better.

DUCHESS
If I had a husband now, this care were quit:
But I intend to make you overseer.
What good deed shall we first remember? Say.

ANTONIO
Begin with that first good deed began i' the world
After man's creation, the sacrament of marriage;
I 'd have you first provide for a good husband;
Give him all.

DUCHESS
All!

ANTONIO
Yes, your excellent self.

DUCHESS
In a winding-sheet?

ANTONIO
In a couple.

DUCHESS
Saint Winifred, that were a strange will!

ANTONIO
'Twere stranger[23] if there were no will in you
To marry again.

DUCHESS
What do you think of marriage?

ANTONIO
I take 't, as those that deny purgatory,

It locally contains or heaven or hell;
There's no third place in 't.

DUCHESS
How do you affect it?

ANTONIO
My banishment, feeding my melancholy,
Would often reason thus.

DUCHESS
Pray, let's hear it.

ANTONIO
Say a man never marry, nor have children,
What takes that from him? Only the bare name
Of being a father, or the weak delight
To see the little wanton ride a-cock-horse
Upon a painted stick, or hear him chatter
Like a taught starling.

DUCHESS
Fie, fie, what's all this?
One of your eyes is blood-shot; use my ring to 't.
They say 'tis very sovereign. 'Twas my wedding-ring,
And I did vow never to part with it
But to my second husband.

ANTONIO
You have parted with it now.

DUCHESS
Yes, to help your eye-sight.

ANTONIO
You have made me stark blind.

DUCHESS
How?

ANTONIO
There is a saucy and ambitious devil
Is dancing in this circle.

DUCHESS
Remove him.

ANTONIO

How?

DUCHESS
There needs small conjuration, when your finger
May do it: thus. Is it fit?

[She puts the ring upon his finger: he kneels.]

ANTONIO
What said you?

DUCHESS
Sir,
This goodly roof of yours is too low built;
I cannot stand upright in 't nor discourse,
Without I raise it higher. Raise yourself;
Or, if you please, my hand to help you: so.

[Raises him.]

ANTONIO
Ambition, madam, is a great man's madness,
That is not kept in chains and close-pent rooms,
But in fair lightsome lodgings, and is girt
With the wild noise of prattling visitants,
Which makes it lunatic beyond all cure.
Conceive not I am so stupid but I aim[24]
Whereto your favours tend: but he 's a fool
That, being a-cold, would thrust his hands i' the fire
To warm them.

DUCHESS
So, now the ground 's broke,
You may discover what a wealthy mine
I make your lord of.

ANTONIO
O my unworthiness!

DUCHESS
You were ill to sell yourself:
This dark'ning of your worth is not like that
Which tradesmen use i' the city; their false lights
Are to rid bad wares off: and I must tell you,
If you will know where breathes a complete man
(I speak it without flattery), turn your eyes,
And progress through yourself.

ANTONIO
Were there nor heaven nor hell,
I should be honest: I have long serv'd virtue,
And ne'er ta'en wages of her.

DUCHESS
Now she pays it.
The misery of us that are born great!
We are forc'd to woo, because none dare woo us;
And as a tyrant doubles with his words,
And fearfully equivocates, so we
Are forc'd to express our violent passions
In riddles and in dreams, and leave the path
Of simple virtue, which was never made
To seem the thing it is not. Go, go brag
You have left me heartless; mine is in your bosom:
I hope 'twill multiply love there. You do tremble:
Make not your heart so dead a piece of flesh,
To fear more than to love me. Sir, be confident:
What is 't distracts you? This is flesh and blood, sir;
'Tis not the figure cut in alabaster
Kneels at my husband's tomb. Awake, awake, man!
I do here put off all vain ceremony,
And only do appear to you a young widow
That claims you for her husband, and, like a widow,
I use but half a blush in 't.

ANTONIO
Truth speak for me;
I will remain the constant sanctuary
Of your good name.

DUCHESS
I thank you, gentle love:
And 'cause you shall not come to me in debt,
Being now my steward, here upon your lips
I sign your Quietus est.[25] This you should have begg'd now.
I have seen children oft eat sweetmeats thus,
As fearful to devour them too soon.

ANTONIO
But for your brothers?

DUCHESS
Do not think of them:
All discord without this circumference
Is only to be pitied, and not fear'd:
Yet, should they know it, time will easily

Scatter the tempest.

ANTONIO
These words should be mine,
And all the parts you have spoke, if some part of it
Would not have savour'd flattery.

DUCHESS
Kneel.

[**CARIOLA** comes from behind the arras.]

ANTONIO
Ha!

DUCHESS
Be not amaz'd; this woman 's of my counsel:
I have heard lawyers say, a contract in a chamber
Per verba [de] presenti[26] is absolute marriage.

[She and **ANTONIO** kneel.]

Bless, heaven, this sacred gordian[27] which let violence
Never untwine!

ANTONIO
And may our sweet affections, like the spheres,
Be still in motion!

DUCHESS
Quickening, and make
The like soft music!

ANTONIO
That we may imitate the loving palms,
Best emblem of a peaceful marriage,
That never bore fruit, divided!

DUCHESS
What can the church force more?

ANTONIO
That fortune may not know an accident,
Either of joy or sorrow, to divide
Our fixed wishes!

DUCHESS
How can the church build faster?[28]

We now are man and wife, and 'tis the church
That must but echo this.—Maid, stand apart:
I now am blind.

ANTONIO
What 's your conceit in this?

DUCHESS
I would have you lead your fortune by the hand
Unto your marriage-bed:
(You speak in me this, for we now are one:)
We 'll only lie and talk together, and plot
To appease my humorous[29] kindred; and if you please,
Like the old tale in ALEXANDER AND LODOWICK,
Lay a naked sword between us, keep us chaste.
O, let me shrowd my blushes in your bosom,
Since 'tis the treasury of all my secrets!

[Exeunt **DUCHESS** and **ANTONIO**]

CARIOLA
Whether the spirit of greatness or of woman
Reign most in her, I know not; but it shows
A fearful madness. I owe her much of pity.

[Exit.]

ACT II

SCENE I [30]

[Enter] **BOSOLA** and **CASTRUCCIO**

BOSOLA
You say you would fain be taken for an eminent courtier?

CASTRUCCIO
'Tis the very main[31] of my ambition.

BOSOLA
Let me see: you have a reasonable good face for 't already, and your night-cap expresses your ears sufficient largely. I would have you learn to twirl the strings of your band with a good grace, and in a set speech, at th' end of every sentence, to hum three or four times, or blow your nose till it smart again, to recover your memory. When you come to be a president in criminal causes, if you smile upon a prisoner, hang him; but if you frown upon him and threaten him, let him be sure to scape the gallows.

CASTRUCCIO
I would be a very merry president.

BOSOLA
Do not sup o' nights; 'twill beget you an admirable wit.

CASTRUCCIO
Rather it would make me have a good stomach to quarrel; for they say, your roaring boys eat meat seldom, and that makes them so valiant. But how shall I know whether the people take me for an eminent fellow?

BOSOLA
I will teach a trick to know it: give out you lie a-dying, and if you hear the common people curse you, be sure you are taken for one of the prime night-caps.[32]

[Enter an **OLD LADY**]

You come from painting now.

OLD LADY
From what?

BOSOLA
Why, from your scurvy face-physic. To behold thee not painted inclines somewhat near a miracle. These in thy face here were deep ruts and foul sloughs the last progress.[33] There was a lady in France that, having had the small-pox, flayed the skin off her face to make it more level; and whereas before she looked like a nutmeg-grater, after she resembled an abortive hedge-hog.

OLD LADY
Do you call this painting?

BOSOLA
No, no, but you call it careening[34] of an old morphewed[35] lady, to make her disembogue[36] again: there's rough-cast phrase to your plastic.[37]

OLD LADY
It seems you are well acquainted with my closet.

BOSOLA
One would suspect it for a shop of witchcraft, to find in it the fat of serpents, spawn of snakes, Jews' spittle, and their young children's ordure; and all these for the face. I would sooner eat a dead pigeon taken from the soles of the feet of one sick of the plague, than kiss one of you fasting. Here are two of you, whose sin of your youth is the very patrimony of the physician; makes him renew his foot-cloth with the spring, and change his high-pric'd courtesan with the fall of the leaf. I do wonder you do not loathe yourselves.
Observe my meditation now.
What thing is in this outward form of man
To be belov'd? We account it ominous,

If nature do produce a colt, or lamb,
A fawn, or goat, in any limb resembling
A man, and fly from 't as a prodigy:
Man stands amaz'd to see his deformity
In any other creature but himself.
But in our own flesh though we bear diseases
Which have their true names only ta'en from beasts,—
As the most ulcerous wolf and swinish measle,—
Though we are eaten up of lice and worms,
And though continually we bear about us
A rotten and dead body, we delight
To hide it in rich tissue: all our fear,
Nay, all our terror, is, lest our physician
Should put us in the ground to be made sweet.—
Your wife 's gone to Rome: you two couple, and get you to
the wells at Lucca to recover your aches. I have other work on foot.

[Exeunt **CASTRUCCIO** and **OLD LADY**]

I observe our duchess
Is sick a-days, she pukes, her stomach seethes,
The fins of her eye-lids look most teeming blue,[38]
She wanes i' the cheek, and waxes fat i' the flank,
And, contrary to our Italian fashion,
Wears a loose-bodied gown: there 's somewhat in 't.
I have a trick may chance discover it,
A pretty one; I have bought some apricocks,
The first our spring yields.

[Enter **ANTONIO** and **DELIO**, talking together apart]

DELIO
And so long since married?
You amaze me.

ANTONIO
Let me seal your lips for ever:
For, did I think that anything but th' air
Could carry these words from you, I should wish
You had no breath at all.—Now, sir, in your contemplation?
You are studying to become a great wise fellow.

BOSOLA
O, sir, the opinion of wisdom is a foul tetter[39] that runs all over a man's body: if simplicity direct us to have no evil, it directs us to a happy being; for the subtlest folly proceeds from the subtlest wisdom: let me be simply honest.

ANTONIO

I do understand your inside.

BOSOLA
Do you so?

ANTONIO
Because you would not seem to appear to th' world
Puff'd up with your preferment, you continue
This out-of-fashion melancholy: leave it, leave it.

BOSOLA
Give me leave to be honest in any phrase, in any compliment whatsoever. Shall I confess myself to you? I look no higher than I can reach: they are the gods that must ride on winged horses. A lawyer's mule of a slow pace will both suit my disposition and business; for, mark me, when a man's mind rides faster than his horse can gallop, they quickly both tire.

ANTONIO
You would look up to heaven, but I think
The devil, that rules i' th' air, stands in your light.

BOSOLA
O, sir, you are lord of the ascendant,[40] chief man with the duchess: a duke was your cousin-german remov'd. Say you were lineally descended from King Pepin, or he himself, what of this? Search the heads of the greatest rivers in the world, you shall find them but bubbles of water. Some would think the souls of princes were brought forth by some more weighty cause than those of meaner persons: they are deceiv'd, there's the same hand to them; the like passions sway them; the same reason that makes a vicar go to law for a tithe-pig, and undo his neighbours, makes them spoil a whole province, and batter down goodly cities with the cannon.

[Enter **DUCHESS** and **LADIES**]

DUCHESS
Your arm, Antonio: do I not grow fat?
I am exceeding short-winded.—Bosola,
I would have you, sir, provide for me a litter;
Such a one as the Duchess of Florence rode in.

BOSOLA
The duchess us'd one when she was great with child.

DUCHESS
I think she did.—Come hither, mend my ruff:
Here, when? thou art such a tedious lady; and
Thy breath smells of lemon-pills: would thou hadst done!
Shall I swoon under thy fingers? I am
So troubled with the mother![41]

BOSOLA [Aside.]

I fear too much.

DUCHESS
I have heard you say that the French courtiers
Wear their hats on 'fore that king.

ANTONIO
I have seen it.

DUCHESS
In the presence?

ANTONIO
Yes.

DUCHESS
Why should not we bring up that fashion?
'Tis ceremony more than duty that consists
In the removing of a piece of felt.
Be you the example to the rest o' th' court;
Put on your hat first.

ANTONIO
You must pardon me:
I have seen, in colder countries than in France,
Nobles stand bare to th' prince; and the distinction
Methought show'd reverently.

BOSOLA
I have a present for your grace.

DUCHESS
For me, sir?

BOSOLA
Apricocks, madam.

DUCHESS
O, sir, where are they?
I have heard of none to-year[42]

BOSOLA [Aside.]
Good; her colour rises.

DUCHESS
Indeed, I thank you: they are wondrous fair ones.
What an unskilful fellow is our gardener!
We shall have none this month.

BOSOLA
Will not your grace pare them?

DUCHESS
No: they taste of musk, methinks; indeed they do.

BOSOLA
I know not: yet I wish your grace had par'd 'em.

DUCHESS
Why?

BOSOLA
I forgot to tell you, the knave gardener,
Only to raise his profit by them the sooner,
Did ripen them in horse-dung.

DUCHESS
O, you jest.—
You shall judge: pray, taste one.

ANTONIO
Indeed, madam,
I do not love the fruit.

DUCHESS
Sir, you are loth
To rob us of our dainties
'Tis a delicate fruit;
They say they are restorative.

BOSOLA
'Tis a pretty art,
This grafting.

DUCHESS
'Tis so; a bettering of nature.

BOSOLA
To make a pippin grow upon a crab,
A damson on a black-thorn.—[Aside.] How greedily she eats them!
A whirlwind strike off these bawd farthingales!
For, but for that and the loose-bodied gown,
I should have discover'd apparently[43]
The young springal[44] cutting a caper in her belly.

DUCHESS

I thank you, Bosola: they were right good ones,
If they do not make me sick.

ANTONIO
How now, madam!

DUCHESS
This green fruit and my stomach are not friends:
How they swell me!

BOSOLA [Aside.]
Nay, you are too much swell'd already.

DUCHESS
O, I am in an extreme cold sweat!

BOSOLA
I am very sorry.

[Exit.]

DUCHESS
Lights to my chamber!—O good Antonio,
I fear I am undone!

DELIO
Lights there, lights!

Exeunt **DUCHESS** and **LADIES**.]

ANTONIO
O my most trusty Delio, we are lost!
I fear she 's fall'n in labour; and there 's left
No time for her remove.

DELIO
Have you prepar'd
Those ladies to attend her; and procur'd
That politic safe conveyance for the midwife
Your duchess plotted?

ANTONIO
I have.

DELIO
Make use, then, of this forc'd occasion.
Give out that Bosola hath poison'd her
With these apricocks; that will give some colour

For her keeping close.

ANTONIO
Fie, fie, the physicians
Will then flock to her.

DELIO
For that you may pretend
She'll use some prepar'd antidote of her own,
Lest the physicians should re-poison her.

ANTONIO
I am lost in amazement: I know not what to think on 't.

[Exeunt.]

SCENE II [45]

[Enter **BOSOLA** and **OLD LADY**.

BOSOLA
So, so, there 's no question but her techiness[46] and most vulturous eating of the apricocks are apparent signs of breeding, now?

OLD LADY
I am in haste, sir.

BOSOLA
There was a young waiting-woman had a monstrous desire to see the glass-house—

OLD LADY
Nay, pray, let me go
I will hear no more
of the glass-house
You are still[47] abusing women!

BOSOLA
Who, I? No; only, by the way now and then, mention your frailties. The orange-tree bears ripe and green fruit and blossoms all together; and some of you give entertainment for pure love, but more for more precious reward. The lusty spring smells well; but drooping autumn tastes well. If we have the same golden showers that rained in the time of Jupiter the thunderer, you have the same Danaes still, to hold up their laps to receive them. Didst thou never study the mathematics?

OLD LADY
What 's that, sir?

BOSOLA
Why, to know the trick how to make a many lines meet in one centre. Go, go, give your foster-daughters good counsel: tell them, that the devil takes delight to hang at a woman's girdle, like a false rusty watch, that she cannot discern how the time passes.

[Exit **OLD LADY**.]

[Enter **ANTONIO**, **RODERIGO**, and **GRISOLAN**]

ANTONIO
Shut up the court-gates.

RODERIGO
Why, sir? What's the danger?

ANTONIO
Shut up the posterns presently, and call
All the officers o' th' court.

GRISOLAN
I shall instantly.

[Exit.]

ANTONIO
Who keeps the key o' th' park-gate?

RODERIGO
Forobosco.

ANTONIO
Let him bring 't presently.

[Re-enter **GRISOLAN** with **SERVANTS**]

FIRST SERVANT
O, gentleman o' th' court, the foulest treason!

BOSOLA [Aside.]
If that these apricocks should be poison'd now,
Without my knowledge?

FIRST SERVANT.
There was taken even now a Switzer in the duchess' bed-chamber—

SECOND SERVANT
A Switzer!

FIRST SERVANT
With a pistol—

SECOND SERVANT
There was a cunning traitor!

FIRST SERVANT.
And all the moulds of his buttons were leaden bullets.

SECOND SERVANT
O wicked cannibal!

FIRST SERVANT
'Twas a French plot, upon my life.

SECOND SERVANT
To see what the devil can do!

ANTONIO
Are all the officers here?

SERVANTS
We are.

ANTONIO
Gentlemen,
We have lost much plate, you know; and but this evening
Jewels, to the value of four thousand ducats,
Are missing in the duchess' cabinet.
Are the gates shut?

SERVANT
Yes.

ANTONIO
'Tis the duchess' pleasure
Each officer be lock'd into his chamber
Till the sun-rising; and to send the keys
Of all their chests and of their outward doors
Into her bed-chamber. She is very sick.

RODERIGO
At her pleasure.

ANTONIO
She entreats you take 't not ill: the innocent
Shall be the more approv'd by it.

BOSOLA
Gentlemen o' the wood-yard, where 's your Switzer now?

FIRST SERVANT
By this hand, 'twas credibly reported by one o' the black guard.[48]

[Exeunt all except **ANTONIO** and **DELIO**]

DELIO
How fares it with the duchess?

ANTONIO
She 's expos'd
Unto the worst of torture, pain, and fear.

DELIO
Speak to her all happy comfort.

ANTONIO
How I do play the fool with mine own danger!
You are this night, dear friend, to post to Rome:
My life lies in your service.

DELIO
Do not doubt me.

ANTONIO
O, 'tis far from me: and yet fear presents me
Somewhat that looks like danger.

DELIO
Believe it,
'Tis but the shadow of your fear, no more:
How superstitiously we mind our evils!
The throwing down salt, or crossing of a hare,
Bleeding at nose, the stumbling of a horse,
Or singing of a cricket, are of power
To daunt whole man in us. Sir, fare you well:
I wish you all the joys of a bless'd father;
And, for my faith, lay this unto your breast,—
Old friends, like old swords, still are trusted best.

[Exit.]

[Enter **CARIOLA**]

CARIOLA
Sir, you are the happy father of a son:

Your wife commends him to you.

ANTONIO
Blessed comfort!—
For heaven' sake, tend her well: I 'll presently[49]
Go set a figure for 's nativity.[50]

[Exeunt.]

SCENE III[51]

[Enter **BOSOLA**, with a dark lantern]

BOSOLA
Sure I did hear a woman shriek: list, ha!
And the sound came, if I receiv'd it right,
From the duchess' lodgings. There 's some stratagem
In the confining all our courtiers
To their several wards: I must have part of it;
My intelligence will freeze else. List, again!
It may be 'twas the melancholy bird,
Best friend of silence and of solitariness,
The owl, that screamed so.—Ha! Antonio!

[Enter **ANTONIO** with a candle, his sword drawn]

ANTONIO
I heard some noise.—Who 's there? What art thou? Speak.

BOSOLA
Antonio, put not your face nor body
To such a forc'd expression of fear;
I am Bosola, your friend.

ANTONIO
Bosola!—
[Aside.] This mole does undermine me.—Heard you not
A noise even now?

BOSOLA
From whence?

ANTONIO
From the duchess' lodging.

BOSOLA

Not I: did you?

ANTONIO
I did, or else I dream'd.

BOSOLA
Let 's walk towards it.

ANTONIO
No: it may be 'twas
But the rising of the wind.

BOSOLA
Very likely.
Methinks 'tis very cold, and yet you sweat:
You look wildly.

ANTONIO
I have been setting a figure[52]
For the duchess' jewels.

BOSOLA
Ah, and how falls your question?
Do you find it radical?[53]

ANTONIO
What 's that to you?
'Tis rather to be question'd what design,
When all men were commanded to their lodgings,
Makes you a night-walker.

BOSOLA
In sooth, I 'll tell you:
Now all the court 's asleep, I thought the devil
Had least to do here; I came to say my prayers;
And if it do offend you I do so,
You are a fine courtier.

ANTONIO [Aside.]
This fellow will undo me.—
You gave the duchess apricocks to-day:
Pray heaven they were not poison'd!

BOSOLA
Poison'd! a Spanish fig
For the imputation!

ANTONIO

Traitors are ever confident
Till they are discover'd. There were jewels stol'n too:
In my conceit, none are to be suspected
More than yourself.

BOSOLA
You are a false steward.

ANTONIO
Saucy slave, I'll pull thee up by the roots.

BOSOLA
May be the ruin will crush you to pieces.

ANTONIO
You are an impudent snake indeed, sir:
Are you scarce warm, and do you show your sting?
You libel[54] well, sir?

BOSOLA
No, sir: copy it out,
And I will set my hand to 't.

ANTONIO [Aside.]
My nose bleeds.
One that were superstitious would count
This ominous, when it merely comes by chance.
Two letters, that are wrought here for my name,[55]
Are drown'd in blood!
Mere accident.—For you, sir, I'll take order
I' the morn you shall be safe.—[Aside.] 'Tis that must colour
Her lying-in.—Sir, this door you pass not:
I do not hold it fit that you come near
The duchess' lodgings, till you have quit yourself.—
[Aside.] The great are like the base, nay, they are the same,
When they seek shameful ways to avoid shame.

[Exit.

BOSOLA
Antonio hereabout did drop a paper:—
Some of your help, false friend.[56]—O, here it is.
What 's here? a child's nativity calculated!
[Reads.]
'The duchess was deliver'd of a son, 'tween the hours twelve and one in the night, Anno Dom. 1504,'—that 's this year—'decimo nono Decembris,'—that 's this night—'taken according to the meridian of Malfi,'—that 's our duchess: happy discovery!—'The lord of the first house being combust in

the ascendant, signifies short life; and Mars being in a human sign, joined to the tail of the Dragon, in the eighth house, doth threaten a violent death. Caetera non scrutantur.'[57]

Why, now 'tis most apparent; this precise fellow
Is the duchess' bawd:—I have it to my wish!
This is a parcel of intelligency[58]
Our courtiers were cas'd up for: it needs must follow
That I must be committed on pretence
Of poisoning her; which I 'll endure, and laugh at.
If one could find the father now! but that
Time will discover. Old Castruccio
I' th' morning posts to Rome: by him I 'll send
A letter that shall make her brothers' galls
O'erflow their livers. This was a thrifty[59] way!
Though lust do mask in ne'er so strange disguise,
She 's oft found witty, but is never wise.

[Exit.]

SCENE IV [60]

[Enter **CARDINAL** and **JULIA**

CARDINAL
Sit: thou art my best of wishes. Prithee, tell me
What trick didst thou invent to come to Rome
Without thy husband?

JULIA
Why, my lord, I told him
I came to visit an old anchorite[61]
Here for devotion.

CARDINAL
Thou art a witty false one,—
I mean, to him.

JULIA
You have prevail'd with me
Beyond my strongest thoughts; I would not now
Find you inconstant.

CARDINAL
Do not put thyself
To such a voluntary torture, which proceeds
Out of your own guilt.

JULIA
How, my lord!

CARDINAL
You fear
My constancy, because you have approv'd[62]
Those giddy and wild turnings in yourself.

JULIA
Did you e'er find them?

CARDINAL
Sooth, generally for women,
A man might strive to make glass malleable,
Ere he should make them fixed.

JULIA
So, my lord.

CARDINAL
We had need go borrow that fantastic glass
Invented by Galileo the Florentine
To view another spacious world i' th' moon,
And look to find a constant woman there.

JULIA
This is very well, my lord.

CARDINAL
Why do you weep?
Are tears your justification? The self-same tears
Will fall into your husband's bosom, lady,
With a loud protestation that you love him
Above the world. Come, I 'll love you wisely,
That 's jealously; since I am very certain
You cannot make me cuckold.

JULIA
I 'll go home
To my husband.

CARDINAL
You may thank me, lady,
I have taken you off your melancholy perch,
Bore you upon my fist, and show'd you game,
And let you fly at it.—I pray thee, kiss me.—
When thou wast with thy husband, thou wast watch'd

Like a tame elephant:—still you are to thank me:—
Thou hadst only kisses from him and high feeding;
But what delight was that? 'Twas just like one
That hath a little fing'ring on the lute,
Yet cannot tune it:—still you are to thank me.

JULIA
You told me of a piteous wound i' th' heart,
And a sick liver, when you woo'd me first,
And spake like one in physic.[63]

CARDINAL
Who 's that?—

[Enter **SERVANT**]

Rest firm, for my affection to thee,
Lightning moves slow to 't.

SERVANT
Madam, a gentleman,
That 's come post from Malfi, desires to see you.

CARDINAL
Let him enter: I 'll withdraw.

[Exit.]

SERVANT
He says
Your husband, old Castruccio, is come to Rome,
Most pitifully tir'd with riding post.

[Exit.]

[Enter **DELIO**]

JULIA [Aside.]
Signior Delio! 'tis one of my old suitors.

DELIO
I was bold to come and see you.

JULIA
Sir, you are welcome.

DELIO
Do you lie here?

JULIA
Sure, your own experience
Will satisfy you no: our Roman prelates
Do not keep lodging for ladies.

DELIO
Very well:
I have brought you no commendations from your husband,
For I know none by him.

JULIA
I hear he 's come to Rome.

DELIO
I never knew man and beast, of a horse and a knight,
So weary of each other. If he had had a good back,
He would have undertook to have borne his horse,
His breech was so pitifully sore.

JULIA
Your laughter
Is my pity.

DELIO
Lady, I know not whether
You want money, but I have brought you some.

JULIA
From my husband?

DELIO
No, from mine own allowance.

JULIA
I must hear the condition, ere I be bound to take it.

DELIO
Look on 't, 'tis gold; hath it not a fine colour?

JULIA
I have a bird more beautiful.

DELIO
Try the sound on 't.

JULIA
A lute-string far exceeds it.

It hath no smell, like cassia or civet;
Nor is it physical,[64] though some fond doctors
Persuade us seethe 't in cullises.[65] I 'll tell you,
This is a creature bred by—

[Re-enter **SERVANT**]

SERVANT
Your husband 's come,
Hath deliver'd a letter to the Duke of Calabria
That, to my thinking, hath put him out of his wits.

[Exit.]

JULIA
Sir, you hear:
Pray, let me know your business and your suit
As briefly as can be.

DELIO
With good speed: I would wish you,
At such time as you are non-resident
With your husband, my mistress.

JULIA
Sir, I 'll go ask my husband if I shall,
And straight return your answer.

[Exit.

DELIO
Very fine!
Is this her wit, or honesty, that speaks thus?
I heard one say the duke was highly mov'd
With a letter sent from Malfi. I do fear
Antonio is betray'd. How fearfully
Shows his ambition now! Unfortunate fortune!
They pass through whirl-pools, and deep woes do shun,
Who the event weigh ere the action 's done.

[Exit.

SCENE V [66]

[Enter **CARDINAL** and **FERDINAND** with a letter

FERDINAND
I have this night digg'd up a mandrake.[67]

CARDINAL
Say you?

FERDINAND
And I am grown mad with 't.

CARDINAL
What 's the prodigy?

FERDINAND
Read there,—a sister damn'd: she 's loose i' the hilts;[68]
Grown a notorious strumpet.

CARDINAL
Speak lower.

FERDINAND
Lower!
Rogues do not whisper 't now, but seek to publish 't
(As servants do the bounty of their lords)
Aloud; and with a covetous searching eye,
To mark who note them. O, confusion seize her!
She hath had most cunning bawds to serve her turn,
And more secure conveyances for lust
Than towns of garrison for service.

CARDINAL
Is 't possible?
Can this be certain?

FERDINAND
Rhubarb, O, for rhubarb
To purge this choler! Here 's the cursed day
To prompt my memory; and here 't shall stick
Till of her bleeding heart I make a sponge
To wipe it out.

CARDINAL
Why do you make yourself
So wild a tempest?

FERDINAND
Would I could be one,
That I might toss her palace 'bout her ears,
Root up her goodly forests, blast her meads,

And lay her general territory as waste
As she hath done her honours.

CARDINAL
Shall our blood,
The royal blood of Arragon and Castile,
Be thus attainted?

FERDINAND
Apply desperate physic:
We must not now use balsamum, but fire,
The smarting cupping-glass, for that 's the mean
To purge infected blood, such blood as hers.
There is a kind of pity in mine eye,—
I 'll give it to my handkercher; and now 'tis here,
I 'll bequeath this to her bastard.

CARDINAL
What to do?

FERDINAND
Why, to make soft lint for his mother's wounds,
When I have hew'd her to pieces.

CARDINAL
Curs'd creature!
Unequal nature, to place women's hearts
So far upon the left side![69]

FERDINAND
Foolish men,
That e'er will trust their honour in a bark
Made of so slight weak bulrush as is woman,
Apt every minute to sink it!

CARDINAL
Thus ignorance, when it hath purchas'd honour,
It cannot wield it.

FERDINAND
Methinks I see her laughing,—
Excellent hyena! Talk to me somewhat quickly,
Or my imagination will carry me
To see her in the shameful act of sin.

CARDINAL
With whom?

FERDINAND
Happily with some strong-thigh'd bargeman,
Or one o' th' wood-yard that can quoit the sledge[70]
Or toss the bar, or else some lovely squire
That carries coals up to her privy lodgings.

CARDINAL
You fly beyond your reason.

FERDINAND
Go to, mistress!
'Tis not your whore's milk that shall quench my wild-fire,
But your whore's blood.

CARDINAL
How idly shows this rage, which carries you,
As men convey'd by witches through the air,
On violent whirlwinds! This intemperate noise
Fitly resembles deaf men's shrill discourse,
Who talk aloud, thinking all other men
To have their imperfection.

FERDINAND
Have not you
My palsy?

CARDINAL
Yes, but I can be angry
Without this rupture. There is not in nature
A thing that makes man so deform'd, so beastly,
As doth intemperate anger. Chide yourself.
You have divers men who never yet express'd
Their strong desire of rest but by unrest,
By vexing of themselves. Come, put yourself
In tune.

FERDINAND
So I will only study to seem
The thing I am not. I could kill her now,
In you, or in myself; for I do think
It is some sin in us heaven doth revenge
By her.

CARDINAL
Are you stark mad?

FERDINAND
I would have their bodies

Burnt in a coal-pit with the ventage stopp'd,
That their curs'd smoke might not ascend to heaven;
Or dip the sheets they lie in in pitch or sulphur,
Wrap them in 't, and then light them like a match;
Or else to-boil[71] their bastard to a cullis,
And give 't his lecherous father to renew
The sin of his back.

CARDINAL
I 'll leave you.

FERDINAND
Nay, I have done.
I am confident, had I been damn'd in hell,
And should have heard of this, it would have put me
Into a cold sweat. In, in; I 'll go sleep.
Till I know who loves my sister, I 'll not stir:
That known, I 'll find scorpions to string my whips,
And fix her in a general eclipse.

[Exeunt.]

ACT III

SCENE I [72]

[Enter **ANTONIO** and **DELIO**

ANTONIO
Our noble friend, my most beloved Delio!
O, you have been a stranger long at court:
Came you along with the Lord Ferdinand?

DELIO
I did, sir: and how fares your noble duchess?

ANTONIO
Right fortunately well: she 's an excellent
Feeder of pedigrees; since you last saw her,
She hath had two children more, a son and daughter.

DELIO
Methinks 'twas yesterday. Let me but wink,
And not behold your face, which to mine eye
Is somewhat leaner, verily I should dream
It were within this half hour.

ANTONIO
You have not been in law, friend Delio,
Nor in prison, nor a suitor at the court,
Nor begg'd the reversion of some great man's place,
Nor troubled with an old wife, which doth make
Your time so insensibly hasten.

DELIO
Pray, sir, tell me,
Hath not this news arriv'd yet to the ear
Of the lord cardinal?

ANTONIO
I fear it hath:
The Lord Ferdinand, that 's newly come to court,
Doth bear himself right dangerously.

DELIO
Pray, why?

ANTONIO
He is so quiet that he seems to sleep
The tempest out, as dormice do in winter.
Those houses that are haunted are most still
Till the devil be up.

DELIO
What say the common people?

ANTONIO
The common rabble do directly say
She is a strumpet.

DELIO
And your graver heads
Which would be politic, what censure they?

ANTONIO
They do observe I grow to infinite purchase,[73]
The left hand way; and all suppose the duchess
Would amend it, if she could; for, say they,
Great princes, though they grudge their officers
Should have such large and unconfined means
To get wealth under them, will not complain,
Lest thereby they should make them odious
Unto the people. For other obligation
Of love or marriage between her and me

They never dream of.

DELIO
The Lord Ferdinand
Is going to bed.

[Enter **DUCHESS**, **FERDINAND**, and **ATTENDANTS**]

FERDINAND
I 'll instantly to bed,
For I am weary.—I am to bespeak
A husband for you.

DUCHESS
For me, sir! Pray, who is 't?

FERDINAND
The great Count Malatesti.

DUCHESS
Fie upon him!
A count! He 's a mere stick of sugar-candy;
You may look quite through him. When I choose
A husband, I will marry for your honour.

FERDINAND
You shall do well in 't.—How is 't, worthy Antonio?

DUCHESS
But, sir, I am to have private conference with you
About a scandalous report is spread
Touching mine honour.

FERDINAND
Let me be ever deaf to 't:
One of Pasquil's paper-bullets,[74] court-calumny,
A pestilent air, which princes' palaces
Are seldom purg'd of. Yet, say that it were true,
I pour it in your bosom, my fix'd love
Would strongly excuse, extenuate, nay, deny
Faults, were they apparent in you. Go, be safe
In your own innocency.

DUCHESS [Aside.]
O bless'd comfort!
This deadly air is purg'd.

[Exeunt **DUCHESS**, **ANTONIO**, **DELIO**, and **ATTENDANTS**.]

FERDINAND
Her guilt treads on
Hot-burning coulters.[75]

[Enter **BOSOLA**]

Now, Bosola,
How thrives our intelligence?[76]

BOSOLA
Sir, uncertainly:
'Tis rumour'd she hath had three bastards, but
By whom we may go read i' the stars.

FERDINAND
Why, some
Hold opinion all things are written there.

BOSOLA
Yes, if we could find spectacles to read them.
I do suspect there hath been some sorcery
Us'd on the duchess.

FERDINAND
Sorcery! to what purpose?

BOSOLA
To make her dote on some desertless fellow
She shames to acknowledge.

FERDINAND
Can your faith give way
To think there 's power in potions or in charms,
To make us love whether we will or no?

BOSOLA
Most certainly.

FERDINAND
Away! these are mere gulleries,[77] horrid things,
Invented by some cheating mountebanks
To abuse us. Do you think that herbs or charms
Can force the will? Some trials have been made
In this foolish practice, but the ingredients
Were lenitive[78] poisons, such as are of force
To make the patient mad; and straight the witch
Swears by equivocation they are in love.

The witch-craft lies in her rank blood. This night
I will force confession from her. You told me
You had got, within these two days, a false key
Into her bed-chamber.

BOSOLA
I have.

FERDINAND
As I would wish.

BOSOLA
What do you intend to do?

FERDINAND
Can you guess?

BOSOLA
No.

FERDINAND
Do not ask, then:
He that can compass me, and know my drifts,
May say he hath put a girdle 'bout the world,
And sounded all her quick-sands.

BOSOLA
I do not
Think so.

FERDINAND
What do you think, then, pray?

BOSOLA
That you
Are your own chronicle too much, and grossly
Flatter yourself.

FERDINAND
Give me thy hand; I thank thee:
I never gave pension but to flatterers,
Till I entertained thee. Farewell.
That friend a great man's ruin strongly checks,
Who rails into his belief all his defects.

[Exeunt.

SCENE II [79]

[Enter **DUCHESS**, **ANTONIO**, and **CARIOLA**

DUCHESS
Bring me the casket hither, and the glass.—
You get no lodging here to-night, my lord.

ANTONIO
Indeed, I must persuade one.

DUCHESS
Very good:
I hope in time 'twill grow into a custom,
That noblemen shall come with cap and knee
To purchase a night's lodging of their wives.

ANTONIO
I must lie here.

DUCHESS
Must! You are a lord of mis-rule.

ANTONIO
Indeed, my rule is only in the night.

DUCHESS
I 'll stop your mouth.

[Kisses him.]

ANTONIO
Nay, that 's but one; Venus had two soft doves
To draw her chariot; I must have another.—

[She kisses him again.]

When wilt thou marry, Cariola?

CARIOLA
Never, my lord.

ANTONIO
O, fie upon this single life! forgo it.
We read how Daphne, for her peevish flight,[80]
Became a fruitless bay-tree; Syrinx turn'd
To the pale empty reed; Anaxarete

Was frozen into marble: whereas those
Which married, or prov'd kind unto their friends,
Were by a gracious influence transhap'd
Into the olive, pomegranate, mulberry,
Became flowers, precious stones, or eminent stars.

CARIOLA
This is a vain poetry: but I pray you, tell me,
If there were propos'd me, wisdom, riches, and beauty,
In three several young men, which should I choose?

ANTONIO
'Tis a hard question. This was Paris' case,
And he was blind in 't, and there was a great cause;
For how was 't possible he could judge right,
Having three amorous goddesses in view,
And they stark naked? 'Twas a motion
Were able to benight the apprehension
Of the severest counsellor of Europe.
Now I look on both your faces so well form'd,
It puts me in mind of a question I would ask.

CARIOLA
What is 't?

ANTONIO
I do wonder why hard-favour'd ladies,
For the most part, keep worse-favour'd waiting-women
To attend them, and cannot endure fair ones.

DUCHESS
O, that 's soon answer'd.
Did you ever in your life know an ill painter
Desire to have his dwelling next door to the shop
Of an excellent picture-maker? 'Twould disgrace
His face-making, and undo him. I prithee,
When were we so merry?—My hair tangles.

ANTONIO
Pray thee, Cariola, let 's steal forth the room,
And let her talk to herself: I have divers times
Serv'd her the like, when she hath chaf'd extremely.
I love to see her angry. Softly, Cariola.

[Exeunt **ANTONIO** and **CARIOLA**]

DUCHESS
Doth not the colour of my hair 'gin to change?

When I wax gray, I shall have all the court
Powder their hair with arras,[81] to be like me.
You have cause to love me; I ent'red you into my heart

[Enter **FERDINAND** unseen]

Before you would vouchsafe to call for the keys.
We shall one day have my brothers take you napping.
Methinks his presence, being now in court,
Should make you keep your own bed; but you 'll say
Love mix'd with fear is sweetest. I 'll assure you,
You shall get no more children till my brothers
Consent to be your gossips. Have you lost your tongue?
'Tis welcome:
For know, whether I am doom'd to live or die,
I can do both like a prince.

FERDINAND
Die, then, quickly!
Giving her a poniard.
Virtue, where art thou hid? What hideous thing
Is it that doth eclipse thee?

DUCHESS
Pray, sir, hear me.

FERDINAND
Or is it true thou art but a bare name,
And no essential thing?

DUCHESS
Sir—

FERDINAND
Do not speak.

DUCHESS
No, sir:
I will plant my soul in mine ears, to hear you.

FERDINAND
O most imperfect light of human reason,
That mak'st us so unhappy to foresee
What we can least prevent! Pursue thy wishes,
And glory in them: there 's in shame no comfort
But to be past all bounds and sense of shame.

DUCHESS

I pray, sir, hear me: I am married.

FERDINAND
So!

DUCHESS
Happily, not to your liking: but for that,
Alas, your shears do come untimely now
To clip the bird's wings that 's already flown!
Will you see my husband?

FERDINAND
Yes, if I could change
Eyes with a basilisk.

DUCHESS
Sure, you came hither
By his confederacy.

FERDINAND
The howling of a wolf
Is music to thee, screech-owl: prithee, peace.—
Whate'er thou art that hast enjoy'd my sister,
For I am sure thou hear'st me, for thine own sake
Let me not know thee. I came hither prepar'd
To work thy discovery; yet am now persuaded
It would beget such violent effects
As would damn us both. I would not for ten millions
I had beheld thee: therefore use all means
I never may have knowledge of thy name;
Enjoy thy lust still, and a wretched life,
On that condition.—And for thee, vile woman,
If thou do wish thy lecher may grow old
In thy embracements, I would have thee build
Such a room for him as our anchorites
To holier use inhabit. Let not the sun
Shine on him till he 's dead; let dogs and monkeys
Only converse with him, and such dumb things
To whom nature denies use to sound his name;
Do not keep a paraquito, lest she learn it;
If thou do love him, cut out thine own tongue,
Lest it bewray him.

DUCHESS
Why might not I marry?
I have not gone about in this to create
Any new world or custom.

FERDINAND
Thou art undone;
And thou hast ta'en that massy sheet of lead
That hid thy husband's bones, and folded it
About my heart.

DUCHESS
Mine bleeds for 't.

FERDINAND
Thine! thy heart!
What should I name 't unless a hollow bullet
Fill'd with unquenchable wild-fire?

DUCHESS
You are in this
Too strict; and were you not my princely brother,
I would say, too wilful: my reputation
Is safe.

FERDINAND
Dost thou know what reputation is?
I 'll tell thee,—to small purpose, since the instruction
Comes now too late.
Upon a time Reputation, Love, and Death,
Would travel o'er the world; and it was concluded
That they should part, and take three several ways.
Death told them, they should find him in great battles,
Or cities plagu'd with plagues: Love gives them counsel
To inquire for him 'mongst unambitious shepherds,
Where dowries were not talk'd of, and sometimes
'Mongst quiet kindred that had nothing left
By their dead parents: 'Stay,' quoth Reputation,
'Do not forsake me; for it is my nature,
If once I part from any man I meet,
I am never found again.' And so for you:
You have shook hands with Reputation,
And made him invisible. So, fare you well:
I will never see you more.

DUCHESS
Why should only I,
Of all the other princes of the world,
Be cas'd up, like a holy relic? I have youth
And a little beauty.

FERDINAND
So you have some virgins

That are witches. I will never see thee more.

[Exit.]

[Re-enter **ANTONIO** with a pistol, and **CARIOLA**]

DUCHESS
You saw this apparition?

ANTONIO
Yes: we are
Betray'd. How came he hither? I should turn
This to thee, for that.

CARIOLA
Pray, sir, do; and when
That you have cleft my heart, you shall read there
Mine innocence.

DUCHESS
That gallery gave him entrance.

ANTONIO
I would this terrible thing would come again,
That, standing on my guard, I might relate
My warrantable love.—

[She shows the poniard.]

Ha! what means this?

DUCHESS
He left this with me.

ANTONIO
And it seems did wish
You would use it on yourself.

DUCHESS
His action seem'd
To intend so much.

ANTONIO
This hath a handle to 't,
As well as a point: turn it towards him, and
So fasten the keen edge in his rank gall.

[Knocking within.]

How now! who knocks?
More earthquakes?

DUCHESS
I stand
As if a mine beneath my feet were ready
To be blown up.

CARIOLA
'Tis Bosola.

DUCHESS
Away!
O misery! methinks unjust actions
Should wear these masks and curtains, and not we.
You must instantly part hence: I have fashion'd it already.

[Exit **ANTONIO**]

[Enter **BOSOLA**]

BOSOLA
The duke your brother is ta'en up in a whirlwind;
Hath took horse, and 's rid post to Rome.

DUCHESS
So late?

BOSOLA
He told me, as he mounted into the saddle,
You were undone.

DUCHESS
Indeed, I am very near it.

BOSOLA
What 's the matter?

DUCHESS
Antonio, the master of our household,
Hath dealt so falsely with me in 's accounts.
My brother stood engag'd with me for money
Ta'en up of certain Neapolitan Jews,
And Antonio lets the bonds be forfeit.

BOSOLA
Strange!—[Aside.] This is cunning.

DUCHESS
And hereupon
My brother's bills at Naples are protested
Against.—Call up our officers.

BOSOLA
I shall.

[Exit.

[Re-enter **ANTONIO**]

DUCHESS
The place that you must fly to is Ancona:
Hire a house there; I 'll send after you
My treasure and my jewels. Our weak safety
Runs upon enginous wheels:[82] short syllables
Must stand for periods. I must now accuse you
Of such a feigned crime as Tasso calls
Magnanima menzogna, a noble lie,
'Cause it must shield our honours.—Hark! they are coming.

[Re-enter **BOSOLA** and **OFFICERS**]

ANTONIO
Will your grace hear me?

DUCHESS
I have got well by you; you have yielded me
A million of loss: I am like to inherit
The people's curses for your stewardship.
You had the trick in audit-time to be sick,
Till I had sign'd your quietus;[83] and that cur'd you
Without help of a doctor.—Gentlemen,
I would have this man be an example to you all;
So shall you hold my favour; I pray, let him;
For h'as done that, alas, you would not think of,
And, because I intend to be rid of him,
I mean not to publish.—Use your fortune elsewhere.

ANTONIO
I am strongly arm'd to brook my overthrow,
As commonly men bear with a hard year.
I will not blame the cause on 't; but do think
The necessity of my malevolent star
Procures this, not her humour. O, the inconstant
And rotten ground of service! You may see,

'Tis even like him, that in a winter night,
Takes a long slumber o'er a dying fire,
A-loth to part from 't; yet parts thence as cold
As when he first sat down.

DUCHESS
We do confiscate,
Towards the satisfying of your accounts,
All that you have.

ANTONIO
I am all yours; and 'tis very fit
All mine should be so.

DUCHESS
So, sir, you have your pass.

ANTONIO
You may see, gentlemen, what 'tis to serve
A prince with body and soul.

[Exit.]

BOSOLA
Here 's an example for extortion: what moisture is drawn out of the sea, when foul weather comes, pours down, and runs into the sea again.

DUCHESS
I would know what are your opinions
Of this Antonio.

SECOND OFFICER
He could not abide to see a pig's head gaping:
I thought your grace would find him a Jew.

THIRD OFFICER
I would you had been his officer, for your own sake.

FOURTH OFFICER
You would have had more money.

FIRST OFFICER
He stopped his ears with black wool, and to those came to him for money said he was thick of hearing.

SECOND OFFICER
Some said he was an hermaphrodite, for he could not abide a woman.

FOURTH OFFICER

How scurvy proud he would look when the treasury was full! Well, let him go.

FIRST OFFICER
Yes, and the chippings of the buttery fly after him, to scour his gold chain.[84]

DUCHESS
Leave us.

[Exeunt **OFFICERS**.]

What do you think of these?

BOSOLA
That these are rogues that in 's prosperity,
But to have waited on his fortune, could have wish'd
His dirty stirrup riveted through their noses,
And follow'd after 's mule, like a bear in a ring;
Would have prostituted their daughters to his lust;
Made their first-born intelligencers;[85] thought none happy
But such as were born under his blest planet,
And wore his livery: and do these lice drop off now?
Well, never look to have the like again:
He hath left a sort[86] of flattering rogues behind him;
Their doom must follow. Princes pay flatterers
In their own money: flatterers dissemble their vices,
And they dissemble their lies; that 's justice.
Alas, poor gentleman!

DUCHESS
Poor! he hath amply fill'd his coffers.

BOSOLA
Sure, he was too honest. Pluto,[87] the god of riches,
When he 's sent by Jupiter to any man,
He goes limping, to signify that wealth
That comes on God's name comes slowly; but when he's sent
On the devil's errand, he rides post and comes in by scuttles.[88]
Let me show you what a most unvalu'd jewel
You have in a wanton humour thrown away,
To bless the man shall find him. He was an excellent
Courtier and most faithful; a soldier that thought it
As beastly to know his own value too little
As devilish to acknowledge it too much.
Both his virtue and form deserv'd a far better fortune:
His discourse rather delighted to judge itself than show itself:
His breast was fill'd with all perfection,
And yet it seemed a private whisp'ring-room,
It made so little noise of 't.

DUCHESS
But he was basely descended.

BOSOLA
Will you make yourself a mercenary herald,
Rather to examine men's pedigrees than virtues?
You shall want[89] him:
For know an honest statesman to a prince
Is like a cedar planted by a spring;
The spring bathes the tree's root, the grateful tree
Rewards it with his shadow: you have not done so.
I would sooner swim to the Bermoothes on
Two politicians' rotten bladders, tied
Together with an intelligencer's heart-string,
Than depend on so changeable a prince's favour.
Fare thee well, Antonio! Since the malice of the world
Would needs down with thee, it cannot be said yet
That any ill happen'd unto thee, considering thy fall
Was accompanied with virtue.

DUCHESS
O, you render me excellent music!

BOSOLA
Say you?

DUCHESS
This good one that you speak of is my husband.

BOSOLA
Do I not dream? Can this ambitious age
Have so much goodness in 't as to prefer
A man merely for worth, without these shadows
Of wealth and painted honours? Possible?

DUCHESS
I have had three children by him.

BOSOLA
Fortunate lady!
For you have made your private nuptial bed
The humble and fair seminary of peace,
No question but: many an unbenefic'd scholar
Shall pray for you for this deed, and rejoice
That some preferment in the world can yet
Arise from merit. The virgins of your land
That have no dowries shall hope your example

Will raise them to rich husbands. Should you want
Soldiers, 'twould make the very Turks and Moors
Turn Christians, and serve you for this act.
Last, the neglected poets of your time,
In honour of this trophy of a man,
Rais'd by that curious engine, your white hand,
Shall thank you, in your grave, for 't; and make that
More reverend than all the cabinets
Of living princes. For Antonio,
His fame shall likewise flow from many a pen,
When heralds shall want coats to sell to men.

DUCHESS
As I taste comfort in this friendly speech,
So would I find concealment.

BOSOLA
O, the secret of my prince,
Which I will wear on th' inside of my heart!

DUCHESS
You shall take charge of all my coin and jewels,
And follow him; for he retires himself
To Ancona.

BOSOLA
So.

DUCHESS
Whither, within few days,
I mean to follow thee.

BOSOLA
Let me think:
I would wish your grace to feign a pilgrimage
To our Lady of Loretto, scarce seven leagues
From fair Ancona; so may you depart
Your country with more honour, and your flight
Will seem a princely progress, retaining
Your usual train about you.

DUCHESS
Sir, your direction
Shall lead me by the hand.

CARIOLA
In my opinion,
She were better progress to the baths at Lucca,

Or go visit the Spa
In Germany; for, if you will believe me,
I do not like this jesting with religion,
This feigned pilgrimage.

DUCHESS
Thou art a superstitious fool:
Prepare us instantly for our departure.
Past sorrows, let us moderately lament them,
For those to come, seek wisely to prevent them.

[Exeunt **DUCHESS** and **CARIOLA**]

BOSOLA
A politician is the devil's quilted anvil;
He fashions all sins on him, and the blows
Are never heard: he may work in a lady's chamber,
As here for proof. What rests[90] but I reveal
All to my lord? O, this base quality[91]
Of intelligencer! Why, every quality i' the world
Prefers but gain or commendation:
Now, for this act I am certain to be rais'd,
And men that paint weeds to the life are prais'd.

[Exit.]

SCENE III [92]

[Enter **CARDINAL**, **FERDINAND**, **MALATESTI**, **PESCARA**, **DELIO**, and **SILVIO**]

CARDINAL
Must we turn soldier, then?

MALATESTI
The emperor,
Hearing your worth that way, ere you attain'd
This reverend garment, joins you in commission
With the right fortunate soldier the Marquis of Pescara,
And the famous Lannoy.

CARDINAL
He that had the honour
Of taking the French king prisoner?

MALATESTI
The same.

Here 's a plot drawn for a new fortification
At Naples.

FERDINAND
This great Count Malatesti, I perceive,
Hath got employment?

DELIO
No employment, my lord;
A marginal note in the muster-book, that he is
A voluntary lord.

FERDINAND
He 's no soldier.

DELIO
He has worn gun-powder in 's hollow tooth for the tooth-ache.

SILVIO
He comes to the leaguer with a full intent
To eat fresh beef and garlic, means to stay
Till the scent be gone, and straight return to court.

DELIO
He hath read all the late service
As the City-Chronicle relates it;
And keeps two pewterers going, only to express
Battles in model.

SILVIO
Then he 'll fight by the book.

DELIO
By the almanac, I think,
To choose good days and shun the critical;
That 's his mistress' scarf.

SILVIO
Yes, he protests
He would do much for that taffeta.

DELIO
I think he would run away from a battle,
To save it from taking prisoner.

SILVIO
He is horribly afraid
Gun-powder will spoil the perfume on 't.

DELIO
I saw a Dutchman break his pate once
For calling him pot-gun; he made his head
Have a bore in 't like a musket.

SILVIO
I would he had made a touch-hole to 't.
He is indeed a guarded sumpter-cloth,[93]
Only for the remove of the court.

[Enter **BOSOLA**]

PESCARA
Bosola arriv'd! What should be the business?
Some falling-out amongst the cardinals.
These factions amongst great men, they are like
Foxes, when their heads are divided,
They carry fire in their tails, and all the country
About them goes to wrack for 't.

SILVIO
What 's that Bosola?

DELIO
I knew him in Padua,—a fantastical scholar, like such who study to know how many knots was in Hercules' club, of what colour Achilles' beard was, or whether Hector were not troubled with the tooth-ache. He hath studied himself half blear-eyed to know the true symmetry of Caesar's nose by a shoeing-horn; and this he did to gain the name of a speculative man.

PESCARA
Mark Prince Ferdinand:
A very salamander lives in 's eye,
To mock the eager violence of fire.

SILVIO
That cardinal hath made more bad faces with his oppression than ever Michael Angelo made good ones. He lifts up 's nose, like a foul porpoise before a storm.

PESCARA
The Lord Ferdinand laughs.

DELIO
Like a deadly cannon
That lightens ere it smokes.

PESCARA
These are your true pangs of death,

The pangs of life, that struggle with great statesmen.

DELIO
In such a deformed silence witches whisper their charms.

CARDINAL
Doth she make religion her riding-hood
To keep her from the sun and tempest?

FERDINAND
That, that damns her. Methinks her fault and beauty,
Blended together, show like leprosy,
The whiter, the fouler. I make it a question
Whether her beggarly brats were ever christ'ned.

CARDINAL
I will instantly solicit the state of Ancona
To have them banish'd.

FERDINAND
You are for Loretto:
I shall not be at your ceremony; fare you well.—
Write to the Duke of Malfi, my young nephew
She had by her first husband, and acquaint him
With 's mother's honesty.

BOSOLA
I will.

FERDINAND
Antonio!
A slave that only smell'd of ink and counters,
And never in 's life look'd like a gentleman,
But in the audit-time.—Go, go presently,
Draw me out an hundred and fifty of our horse,
And meet me at the foot-bridge.
Exeunt.

SCENE IV

[Enter Two **PILGRIMS** to the Shrine of our Lady of Loretto

FIRST PILGRIM
I have not seen a goodlier shrine than this;
Yet I have visited many.

SECOND PILGRIM

The Cardinal of Arragon
Is this day to resign his cardinal's hat:
His sister duchess likewise is arriv'd
To pay her vow of pilgrimage. I expect
A noble ceremony.

FIRST PILGRIM
No question.—They come.

[Here the ceremony of the Cardinal's instalment, in the habit of a soldier, perform'd in delivering up his cross, hat, robes, and ring, at the shrine, and investing him with sword, helmet, shield, and spurs; then **ANTONIO**, the **DUCHESS** and their children, having presented themselves at the shrine, are, by a form of banishment in dumb-show expressed towards them by the **CARDINAL** and the state of Ancona, banished: during all which ceremony, this ditty is sung, to very solemn music, by divers churchmen: and then exeunt all except the Two **PILGRIMS**.

Arms and honours deck thy story,
To thy fame's eternal glory!
Adverse fortune ever fly thee;
No disastrous fate come nigh thee!

I alone will sing thy praises,
Whom to honour virtue raises,
And thy study, that divine is,
Bent to martial discipline is,
Lay aside all those robes lie by thee;
Crown thy arts with arms, they 'll beautify thee.

O worthy of worthiest name, adorn'd in this manner,
Lead bravely thy forces on under war's warlike banner!
O, mayst thou prove fortunate in all martial courses!
Guide thou still by skill in arts and forces!
Victory attend thee nigh, whilst fame sings loud thy powers;
Triumphant conquest crown thy head, and blessings pour down showers![94]

FIRST PILGRIM.
Here 's a strange turn of state! who would have thought
So great a lady would have match'd herself
Unto so mean a person? Yet the cardinal
Bears himself much too cruel.

SECOND PILGRIM
They are banish'd.

FIRST PILGRIM
But I would ask what power hath this state
Of Ancona to determine of a free prince?

SECOND PILGRIM
They are a free state, sir, and her brother show'd
How that the Pope, fore-hearing of her looseness,
Hath seiz'd into th' protection of the church
The dukedom which she held as dowager.

FIRST PILGRIM
But by what justice?

SECOND PILGRIM
Sure, I think by none,
Only her brother's instigation.

FIRST PILGRIM
What was it with such violence he took
Off from her finger?

SECOND PILGRIM
'Twas her wedding-ring;
Which he vow'd shortly he would sacrifice
To his revenge.

FIRST PILGRIM
Alas, Antonio!
If that a man be thrust into a well,
No matter who sets hand to 't, his own weight
Will bring him sooner to th' bottom. Come, let 's hence.
Fortune makes this conclusion general,
All things do help th' unhappy man to fall.

Exeunt.

SCENE V [95]

[Enter **DUCHESS, ANTONIO, CHILDREN, CARIOLA,** and **SERVANTS.**]

DUCHESS
Banish'd Ancona!

ANTONIO
Yes, you see what power
Lightens in great men's breath.

DUCHESS
Is all our train
Shrunk to this poor remainder?

ANTONIO
These poor men
Which have got little in your service, vow
To take your fortune: but your wiser buntings,[96]
Now they are fledg'd, are gone.

DUCHESS
They have done wisely.
This puts me in mind of death: physicians thus,
With their hands full of money, use to give o'er
Their patients.

ANTONIO
Right the fashion of the world:
From decay'd fortunes every flatterer shrinks;
Men cease to build where the foundation sinks.

DUCHESS
I had a very strange dream to-night.

ANTONIO
What was 't?

DUCHESS
Methought I wore my coronet of state,
And on a sudden all the diamonds
Were chang'd to pearls.

ANTONIO
My interpretation
Is, you 'll weep shortly; for to me the pearls
Do signify your tears.

DUCHESS
The birds that live i' th' field
On the wild benefit of nature live
Happier than we; for they may choose their mates,
And carol their sweet pleasures to the spring.

[Enter **BOSOLA** with a letter]

BOSOLA
You are happily o'erta'en.

DUCHESS
From my brother?

BOSOLA
Yes, from the Lord Ferdinand your brother
All love and safety.

DUCHESS
Thou dost blanch mischief,
Would'st make it white. See, see, like to calm weather
At sea before a tempest, false hearts speak fair
To those they intend most mischief.
[Reads.] 'Send Antonio to me; I want his head in a business.'
A politic equivocation!
He doth not want your counsel, but your head;
That is, he cannot sleep till you be dead.
And here 's another pitfall that 's strew'd o'er
With roses; mark it, 'tis a cunning one:
[Reads.]
'I stand engaged for your husband for several debts at Naples: let not that trouble him; I had rather have his heart than his money':—
And I believe so too.

BOSOLA
What do you believe?

DUCHESS
That he so much distrusts my husband's love,
He will by no means believe his heart is with him
Until he see it: the devil is not cunning enough
To circumvent us In riddles.

BOSOLA
Will you reject that noble and free league
Of amity and love which I present you?

DUCHESS
Their league is like that of some politic kings,
Only to make themselves of strength and power
To be our after-ruin; tell them so.

BOSOLA
And what from you?

ANTONIO
Thus tell him; I will not come.

BOSOLA
And what of this?

ANTONIO

My brothers have dispers'd
Bloodhounds abroad; which till I hear are muzzl'd,
No truce, though hatch'd with ne'er such politic skill,
Is safe, that hangs upon our enemies' will.
I 'll not come at them.

BOSOLA
This proclaims your breeding.
Every small thing draws a base mind to fear,
As the adamant draws iron. Fare you well, sir;
You shall shortly hear from 's.

[Exit.]

DUCHESS
I suspect some ambush;
Therefore by all my love I do conjure you
To take your eldest son, and fly towards Milan.
Let us not venture all this poor remainder
In one unlucky bottom.

ANTONIO
You counsel safely.
Best of my life, farewell. Since we must part,
Heaven hath a hand in 't; but no otherwise
Than as some curious artist takes in sunder
A clock or watch, when it is out of frame,
To bring 't in better order.

DUCHESS
I know not which is best,
To see you dead, or part with you.—Farewell, boy:
Thou art happy that thou hast not understanding
To know thy misery; for all our wit
And reading brings us to a truer sense
Of sorrow.—In the eternal church, sir,
I do hope we shall not part thus.

ANTONIO
O, be of comfort!
Make patience a noble fortitude,
And think not how unkindly we are us'd:
Man, like to cassia, is prov'd best, being bruis'd.

DUCHESS
Must I, like to slave-born Russian,
Account it praise to suffer tyranny?
And yet, O heaven, thy heavy hand is in 't!

I have seen my little boy oft scourge his top,
And compar'd myself to 't: naught made me e'er
Go right but heaven's scourge-stick.

ANTONIO
Do not weep:
Heaven fashion'd us of nothing; and we strive
To bring ourselves to nothing.—Farewell, Cariola,
And thy sweet armful.—If I do never see thee more,
Be a good mother to your little ones,
And save them from the tiger: fare you well.

DUCHESS
Let me look upon you once more, for that speech
Came from a dying father. Your kiss is colder
Than that I have seen an holy anchorite
Give to a dead man's skull.

ANTONIO
My heart is turn'd to a heavy lump of lead,
With which I sound my danger: fare you well.

[Exeunt **ANTONIO** and his **SON**.]

DUCHESS
My laurel is all withered.

CARIOLA
Look, madam, what a troop of armed men
Make toward us!

[Re-enter **BOSOLA** visarded, with a **GUARD**.]

DUCHESS
O, they are very welcome:
When Fortune's wheel is over-charg'd with princes,
The weight makes it move swift: I would have my ruin
Be sudden.—I am your adventure, am I not?

BOSOLA
You are: you must see your husband no more.

DUCHESS
What devil art thou that counterfeit'st heaven's thunder?

BOSOLA
Is that terrible? I would have you tell me whether
Is that note worse that frights the silly birds

Out of the corn, or that which doth allure them
To the nets? You have heark'ned to the last too much.

DUCHESS
O misery! like to a rusty o'ercharg'd cannon,
Shall I never fly in pieces?—Come, to what prison?

BOSOLA
To none.

DUCHESS
Whither, then?

BOSOLA
To your palace.

DUCHESS
I have heard
That Charon's boat serves to convey all o'er
The dismal lake, but brings none back again.

BOSOLA
Your brothers mean you safety and pity.

DUCHESS
Pity!
With such a pity men preserve alive
Pheasants and quails, when they are not fat enough
To be eaten.

BOSOLA
These are your children?

DUCHESS
Yes.

BOSOLA
Can they prattle?

DUCHESS
No:
But I intend, since they were born accurs'd,
Curses shall be their first language.

BOSOLA
Fie, madam!
Forget this base, low fellow—

DUCHESS
Were I a man,
I 'd beat that counterfeit face[97] into thy other.

BOSOLA
One of no birth.

DUCHESS
Say that he was born mean,
Man is most happy when 's own actions
Be arguments and examples of his virtue.

BOSOLA
A barren, beggarly virtue.

DUCHESS
I prithee, who is greatest? Can you tell?
Sad tales befit my woe: I 'll tell you one.
A salmon, as she swam unto the sea.
Met with a dog-fish, who encounters her
With this rough language; 'Why art thou so bold
To mix thyself with our high state of floods,
Being no eminent courtier, but one
That for the calmest and fresh time o' th' year
Dost live in shallow rivers, rank'st thyself
With silly smelts and shrimps? And darest thou
Pass by our dog-ship without reverence?'
'O,' quoth the salmon, 'sister, be at peace:
Thank Jupiter we both have pass'd the net!
Our value never can be truly known,
Till in the fisher's basket we be shown:
I' th' market then my price may be the higher,
Even when I am nearest to the cook and fire.'
So to great men the moral may be stretched;
Men oft are valu'd high, when they're most wretched.—
But come, whither you please. I am arm'd 'gainst misery;
Bent to all sways of the oppressor's will:
There 's no deep valley but near some great hill.

[Exeunt.]

ACT IV

SCENE I [98]

[Enter **FERDINAND** and **BOSOLA**]

FERDINAND
How doth our sister duchess bear herself
In her imprisonment?

BOSOLA
Nobly: I 'll describe her.
She 's sad as one long us'd to 't, and she seems
Rather to welcome the end of misery
Than shun it; a behaviour so noble
As gives a majesty to adversity:
You may discern the shape of loveliness
More perfect in her tears than in her smiles:
She will muse for hours together; and her silence,
Methinks, expresseth more than if she spake.

FERDINAND
Her melancholy seems to be fortified
With a strange disdain.

BOSOLA
'Tis so; and this restraint,
Like English mastives that grow fierce with tying,
Makes her too passionately apprehend
Those pleasures she is kept from.

FERDINAND
Curse upon her!
I will no longer study in the book
Of another's heart. Inform her what I told you.

[Exit.]

[Enter **DUCHESS** and **ATTENDANTS**]

BOSOLA
All comfort to your grace!

DUCHESS
I will have none.
Pray thee, why dost thou wrap thy poison'd pills
In gold and sugar?

BOSOLA
Your elder brother, the Lord Ferdinand,
Is come to visit you, and sends you word,
'Cause once he rashly made a solemn vow
Never to see you more, he comes i' th' night;

And prays you gently neither torch nor taper
Shine in your chamber. He will kiss your hand,
And reconcile himself; but for his vow
He dares not see you.

DUCHESS
At his pleasure.—
Take hence the lights.—He 's come.

[Exeunt **ATTENDANTS** with lights.]

[Enter **FERDINAND**]

FERDINAND
Where are you?

DUCHESS
Here, sir.

FERDINAND
This darkness suits you well.

DUCHESS
I would ask you pardon.

FERDINAND
You have it;
For I account it the honorabl'st revenge,
Where I may kill, to pardon.—Where are your cubs?

DUCHESS
Whom?

FERDINAND
Call them your children;
For though our national law distinguish bastards
From true legitimate issue, compassionate nature
Makes them all equal.

DUCHESS
Do you visit me for this?
You violate a sacrament o' th' church
Shall make you howl in hell for 't.

FERDINAND
It had been well,
Could you have liv'd thus always; for, indeed,
You were too much i' th' light:—but no more;

I come to seal my peace with you. Here 's a hand
Gives her a dead man's hand.
To which you have vow'd much love; the ring upon 't
You gave.

DUCHESS
I affectionately kiss it.

FERDINAND
Pray, do, and bury the print of it in your heart.
I will leave this ring with you for a love-token;
And the hand as sure as the ring; and do not doubt
But you shall have the heart too. When you need a friend,
Send it to him that ow'd it; you shall see
Whether he can aid you.

DUCHESS
You are very cold:
I fear you are not well after your travel.—
Ha! lights!—O, horrible!

FERDINAND
Let her have lights enough.

[Exit.]

DUCHESS
What witchcraft doth he practise, that he hath left
A dead man's hand here?

[Here is discovered, behind a traverse,[99] the artificial figures of **ANTONIO** and his **CHILDREN**, appearing as if they were dead.]

BOSOLA
Look you, here 's the piece from which 'twas ta'en.
He doth present you this sad spectacle,
That, now you know directly they are dead,
Hereafter you may wisely cease to grieve
For that which cannot be recovered.

DUCHESS
There is not between heaven and earth one wish
I stay for after this. It wastes me more
Than were 't my picture, fashion'd out of wax,
Stuck with a magical needle, and then buried
In some foul dunghill; and yon 's an excellent property
For a tyrant, which I would account mercy.

BOSOLA
What 's that?

DUCHESS
If they would bind me to that lifeless trunk,
And let me freeze to death.

BOSOLA
Come, you must live.

DUCHESS
That 's the greatest torture souls feel in hell,
In hell, that they must live, and cannot die.
Portia,[100] I 'll new kindle thy coals again,
And revive the rare and almost dead example
Of a loving wife.

BOSOLA
O, fie! despair? Remember
You are a Christian.

DUCHESS
The church enjoins fasting:
I 'll starve myself to death.

BOSOLA
Leave this vain sorrow.
Things being at the worst begin to mend: the bee
When he hath shot his sting into your hand,
May then play with your eye-lid.

DUCHESS
Good comfortable fellow,
Persuade a wretch that 's broke upon the wheel
To have all his bones new set; entreat him live
To be executed again. Who must despatch me?
I account this world a tedious theatre,
For I do play a part in 't 'gainst my will.

BOSOLA
Come, be of comfort; I will save your life.

DUCHESS
Indeed, I have not leisure to tend so small a business.

BOSOLA
Now, by my life, I pity you.

DUCHESS
Thou art a fool, then,
To waste thy pity on a thing so wretched
As cannot pity itself. I am full of daggers.
Puff, let me blow these vipers from me.

[Enter **SERVANT**]

What are you?

SERVANT
One that wishes you long life.

DUCHESS
I would thou wert hang'd for the horrible curse
Thou hast given me: I shall shortly grow one
Of the miracles of pity. I 'll go pray;—

[Exit **SERVANT**.]

No, I 'll go curse.

BOSOLA
O, fie!

DUCHESS
I could curse the stars.

BOSOLA
O, fearful!

DUCHESS
And those three smiling seasons of the year
Into a Russian winter; nay, the world
To its first chaos.

BOSOLA
Look you, the stars shine still.

DUCHESS
O, but you must
Remember, my curse hath a great way to go.—
Plagues, that make lanes through largest families,
Consume them!—

BOSOLA
Fie, lady!

DUCHESS
Let them, like tyrants,
Never be remembered but for the ill they have done;
Let all the zealous prayers of mortified
Churchmen forget them!—

BOSOLA
O, uncharitable!

DUCHESS
Let heaven a little while cease crowning martyrs,
To punish them!—
Go, howl them this, and say, I long to bleed:
It is some mercy when men kill with speed.

[Exit.]

[Re-enter **FERDINAND**]

FERDINAND
Excellent, as I would wish; she 's plagu'd in art.[101]
These presentations are but fram'd in wax
By the curious master in that quality,[102]
Vincentio Lauriola, and she takes them
For true substantial bodies.

BOSOLA
Why do you do this?

FERDINAND
To bring her to despair.

BOSOLA
Faith, end here,
And go no farther in your cruelty:
Send her a penitential garment to put on
Next to her delicate skin, and furnish her
With beads and prayer-books.

FERDINAND
Damn her! that body of hers.
While that my blood run pure in 't, was more worth
Than that which thou wouldst comfort, call'd a soul.
I will send her masques of common courtezans,
Have her meat serv'd up by bawds and ruffians,
And, 'cause she 'll needs be mad, I am resolv'd
To move forth the common hospital
All the mad-folk, and place them near her lodging;

There let them practise together, sing and dance,
And act their gambols to the full o' th' moon:
If she can sleep the better for it, let her.
Your work is almost ended.

BOSOLA
Must I see her again?

FERDINAND
Yes.

BOSOLA
Never.

FERDINAND
You must.

BOSOLA
Never in mine own shape;
That 's forfeited by my intelligence[103]
And this last cruel lie: when you send me next,
The business shall be comfort.

FERDINAND
Very likely;
Thy pity is nothing of kin to thee, Antonio
Lurks about Milan: thou shalt shortly thither,
To feed a fire as great as my revenge,
Which nev'r will slack till it hath spent his fuel:
Intemperate agues make physicians cruel.

[Exeunt.

SCENE II [104]

[Enter] **DUCHESS** and **CARIOLA**

DUCHESS
What hideous noise was that?

CARIOLA
'Tis the wild consort[105]
Of madmen, lady, which your tyrant brother
Hath plac'd about your lodging. This tyranny,
I think, was never practis'd till this hour.

DUCHESS
Indeed, I thank him. Nothing but noise and folly
Can keep me in my right wits; whereas reason
And silence make me stark mad. Sit down;
Discourse to me some dismal tragedy.

CARIOLA
O, 'twill increase your melancholy!

DUCHESS
Thou art deceiv'd:
To hear of greater grief would lessen mine.
This is a prison?

CARIOLA
Yes, but you shall live
To shake this durance off.

DUCHESS
Thou art a fool:
The robin-red-breast and the nightingale
Never live long in cages.

CARIOLA
Pray, dry your eyes.
What think you of, madam?

DUCHESS
Of nothing;
When I muse thus, I sleep.

CARIOLA
Like a madman, with your eyes open?

DUCHESS
Dost thou think we shall know one another
In th' other world?

CARIOLA
Yes, out of question.

DUCHESS
O, that it were possible we might
But hold some two days' conference with the dead!
From them I should learn somewhat, I am sure,
I never shall know here. I'll tell thee a miracle:
I am not mad yet, to my cause of sorrow:
Th' heaven o'er my head seems made of molten brass,

The earth of flaming sulphur, yet I am not mad.
I am acquainted with sad misery
As the tann'd galley-slave is with his oar;
Necessity makes me suffer constantly,
And custom makes it easy. Who do I look like now?

CARIOLA
Like to your picture in the gallery,
A deal of life in show, but none in practice;
Or rather like some reverend monument
Whose ruins are even pitied.

DUCHESS
Very proper;
And Fortune seems only to have her eye-sight
To behold my tragedy.—How now!
What noise is that?

[Enter **SERVANT**]

SERVANT
I am come to tell you
Your brother hath intended you some sport.
A great physician, when the Pope was sick
Of a deep melancholy, presented him
With several sorts[106] of madmen, which wild object
Being full of change and sport, forc'd him to laugh,
And so the imposthume[107] broke: the self-same cure
The duke intends on you.

DUCHESS
Let them come in.

SERVANT
There 's a mad lawyer; and a secular priest;
A doctor that hath forfeited his wits
By jealousy; an astrologian
That in his works said such a day o' the month
Should be the day of doom, and, failing of 't,
Ran mad; an English tailor craz'd i' the brain
With the study of new fashions; a gentleman-usher
Quite beside himself with care to keep in mind
The number of his lady's salutations
Or 'How do you,' she employ'd him in each morning;
A farmer, too, an excellent knave in grain,[108]
Mad 'cause he was hind'red transportation:[109]
And let one broker that 's mad loose to these,
You'd think the devil were among them.

DUCHESS
Sit, Cariola.—Let them loose when you please,
For I am chain'd to endure all your tyranny.

[Enter **MADMEN**]

[Here by a **MADMAN** this song is sung to a dismal kind of music

O, let us howl some heavy note,
Some deadly dogged howl,
Sounding as from the threatening throat
Of beasts and fatal fowl!
As ravens, screech-owls, bulls, and bears,
We 'll bell, and bawl our parts,
Till irksome noise have cloy'd your ears
And corrosiv'd your hearts.
At last, whenas our choir wants breath,
Our bodies being blest,
We 'll sing, like swans, to welcome death,
And die in love and rest.

FIRST MADMAN
Doom's-day not come yet! I 'll draw it nearer by a perspective,[110] or make a glass that shall set all the world on fire upon an instant. I cannot sleep; my pillow is stuffed with a litter of porcupines.

SECOND MADMAN
Hell is a mere glass-house, where the devils are continually blowing up women's souls on hollow irons, and the fire never goes out.

FIRST MADMAN
I have skill in heraldry.

SECOND MADMAN
Hast?

FIRST MADMAN
You do give for your crest a woodcock's head with the brains picked out on 't; you are a very ancient gentleman.

THIRD MADMAN
Greek is turned Turk: we are only to be saved by the Helvetian translation.[111]

FIRST MADMAN
Come on, sir, I will lay the law to you.

SECOND MADMAN
O, rather lay a corrosive: the law will eat to the bone.

THIRD MADMAN
He that drinks but to satisfy nature is damn'd.

FOURTH MADMAN
If I had my glass here, I would show a sight should make all the women here call me mad doctor.

FIRST MADMAN
What 's he? a rope-maker?

SECOND MADMAN
No, no, no, a snuffling knave that, while he shows the tombs, will have his hand in a wench's placket. [112]

THIRD MADMAN
Woe to the caroche[113] that brought home my wife from the masque at three o'clock in the morning! It had a large feather-bed in it.

FOURTH MADMAN
I have pared the devil's nails forty times, roasted them in raven's eggs, and cured agues with them.

THIRD MADMAN
Get me three hundred milch-bats, to make possets[114] to procure sleep.

FOURTH MADMAN
All the college may throw their caps at me:
I have made a soap-boiler costive; it was my masterpiece.

Here the dance, consisting of Eight **MADMEN**, with music answerable thereunto; after which, **BOSOLA**, like an old man, enters.

DUCHESS
Is he mad too?

SERVANT
Pray, question him. I 'll leave you.

[Exeunt **SERVANT** and **MADMEN**.]

BOSOLA
I am come to make thy tomb.

DUCHESS
Ha! my tomb!
Thou speak'st as if I lay upon my death-bed,
Gasping for breath. Dost thou perceive me sick?

BOSOLA

Yes, and the more dangerously, since thy sickness is insensible.

DUCHESS
Thou art not mad, sure: dost know me?

BOSOLA
Yes.

DUCHESS
Who am I?

BOSOLA
Thou art a box of worm-seed, at best but a salvatory [115] of green mummy.[116] What 's this flesh? a little crudded[117] milk, fantastical puff-paste. Our bodies are weaker than those paper-prisons boys use to keep flies in; more contemptible, since ours is to preserve earth-worms. Didst thou ever see a lark in a cage? Such is the soul in the body: this world is like her little turf of grass, and the heaven o'er our heads like her looking-glass, only gives us a miserable knowledge of the small compass of our prison.

DUCHESS
Am not I thy duchess?

BOSOLA
Thou art some great woman, sure, for riot begins to sit on thy forehead (clad in gray hairs) twenty years sooner than on a merry milk-maid's. Thou sleepest worse than if a mouse should be forced to take up her lodging in a cat's ear: a little infant that breeds its teeth, should it lie with thee, would cry out, as if thou wert the more unquiet bedfellow.

DUCHESS
I am Duchess of Malfi still.

BOSOLA
That makes thy sleep so broken:
Glories, like glow-worms, afar off shine bright,
But, look'd to near, have neither heat nor light.

DUCHESS
Thou art very plain.

BOSOLA
My trade is to flatter the dead, not the living;
I am a tomb-maker.

DUCHESS
And thou comest to make my tomb?

BOSOLA
Yes.

DUCHESS
Let me be a little merry:—of what stuff wilt thou make it?

BOSOLA
Nay, resolve me first, of what fashion?

DUCHESS
Why, do we grow fantastical on our deathbed?
Do we affect fashion in the grave?

BOSOLA
Most ambitiously
Princes' images on their tombs do not lie, as they were wont, seeming to pray up to heaven; but with their hands under their cheeks, as if they died of the tooth-ache. They are not carved with their eyes fix'd upon the stars, but as their minds were wholly bent upon the world, the selfsame way they seem to turn their faces.

DUCHESS
Let me know fully therefore the effect
Of this thy dismal preparation,
This talk fit for a charnel.

BOSOLA
Now I shall:—

[Enter **EXECUTIONERS**, with a coffin, cords, and a bell]

Here is a present from your princely brothers;
And may it arrive welcome, for it brings
Last benefit, last sorrow.

DUCHESS
Let me see it:
I have so much obedience in my blood,
I wish it in their veins to do them good.

BOSOLA
This is your last presence-chamber.

CARIOLA
O my sweet lady!

DUCHESS
Peace; it affrights not me.

BOSOLA
I am the common bellman
That usually is sent to condemn'd persons

The night before they suffer.

DUCHESS
Even now thou said'st
Thou wast a tomb-maker.

BOSOLA
'Twas to bring you
By degrees to mortification. Listen.
Hark, now everything is still,
The screech-owl and the whistler shrill
Call upon our dame aloud,
And bid her quickly don her shroud!
Much you had of land and rent;
Your length in clay 's now competent:
A long war disturb'd your mind;
Here your perfect peace is sign'd.
Of what is 't fools make such vain keeping?
Sin their conception, their birth weeping,
Their life a general mist of error,
Their death a hideous storm of terror.
Strew your hair with powders sweet,
Don clean linen, bathe your feet,
And (the foul fiend more to check)
A crucifix let bless your neck.
'Tis now full tide 'tween night and day;
End your groan, and come away.

CARIOLA
Hence, villains, tyrants, murderers! Alas!
What will you do with my lady?—Call for help!

DUCHESS
To whom? To our next neighbours? They are mad-folks.

BOSOLA
Remove that noise.

DUCHESS
Farewell, Cariola.
In my last will I have not much to give:
A many hungry guests have fed upon me;
Thine will be a poor reversion.

CARIOLA
I will die with her.

DUCHESS

I pray thee, look thou giv'st my little boy
Some syrup for his cold, and let the girl
Say her prayers ere she sleep.

[**CARIOLA** is forced out by the **EXECUTIONERS**.]

Now what you please:
What death?

BOSOLA
Strangling; here are your executioners.

DUCHESS
I forgive them:
The apoplexy, catarrh, or cough o' th' lungs,
Would do as much as they do.

BOSOLA
Doth not death fright you?

DUCHESS
Who would be afraid on 't,
Knowing to meet such excellent company
In th' other world?

BOSOLA
Yet, methinks,
The manner of your death should much afflict you:
This cord should terrify you.

DUCHESS
Not a whit:
What would it pleasure me to have my throat cut
With diamonds? or to be smothered
With cassia? or to be shot to death with pearls?
I know death hath ten thousand several doors
For men to take their exits; and 'tis found
They go on such strange geometrical hinges,
You may open them both ways: any way, for heaven-sake,
So I were out of your whispering. Tell my brothers
That I perceive death, now I am well awake,
Best gift is they can give or I can take.
I would fain put off my last woman's-fault,
I 'd not be tedious to you.

FIRST EXECUTIONER
We are ready.

DUCHESS
Dispose my breath how please you; but my body
Bestow upon my women, will you?

FIRST EXECUTIONER
Yes.

DUCHESS
Pull, and pull strongly, for your able strength
Must pull down heaven upon me:—
Yet stay; heaven-gates are not so highly arch'd
As princes' palaces; they that enter there
Must go upon their knees

[Kneels]

—Come, violent death,
Serve for mandragora to make me sleep!—
Go tell my brothers, when I am laid out,
They then may feed in quiet.
They strangle her.

BOSOLA
Where 's the waiting-woman??
Fetch her: some other strangle the children.

[Enter **CARIOLA**]

Look you, there sleeps your mistress.

CARIOLA
O, you are damn'd
Perpetually for this! My turn is next;
Is 't not so ordered?

BOSOLA
Yes, and I am glad
You are so well prepar'd for 't.

CARIOLA
You are deceiv'd, sir,
I am not prepar'd for 't, I will not die;
I will first come to my answer,[118] and know
How I have offended.

BOSOLA
Come, despatch her.—
You kept her counsel; now you shall keep ours.

CARIOLA
I will not die, I must not; I am contracted
To a young gentleman.

FIRST EXECUTIONER
Here 's your wedding-ring.

CARIOLA
Let me but speak with the duke. I 'll discover
Treason to his person.

BOSOLA
Delays:—throttle her.

FIRST EXECUTIONER
She bites and scratches.

CARIOLA
If you kill me now,
I am damn'd; I have not been at confession
This two years.

BOSOLA [To **EXECUTIONERS**.]
When?[119]

CARIOLA
I am quick with child.

BOSOLA
Why, then,
Your credit 's saved.

[**EXECUTIONERS** strangle **CARIOLA**]

Bear her into the next room;
Let these lie still.

[Exeunt the **EXECUTIONERS** with the body of **CARIOLA**]

[Enter **FERDINAND**]

FERDINAND
Is she dead?

BOSOLA
She is what
You 'd have her. But here begin your pity:

Shows the Children strangled.
Alas, how have these offended?

FERDINAND
The death
Of young wolves is never to be pitied.

BOSOLA
Fix your eye here.

FERDINAND
Constantly.

BOSOLA
Do you not weep?
Other sins only speak; murder shrieks out.
The element of water moistens the earth,
But blood flies upwards and bedews the heavens.

FERDINAND
Cover her face; mine eyes dazzle: she died young.

BOSOLA
I think not so; her infelicity
Seem'd to have years too many.

FERDINAND
She and I were twins;
And should I die this instant, I had liv'd
Her time to a minute.

BOSOLA
It seems she was born first:
You have bloodily approv'd the ancient truth,
That kindred commonly do worse agree
Than remote strangers.

FERDINAND
Let me see her face
Again. Why didst thou not pity her? What
An excellent honest man mightst thou have been,
If thou hadst borne her to some sanctuary!
Or, bold in a good cause, oppos'd thyself,
With thy advanced sword above thy head,
Between her innocence and my revenge!
I bade thee, when I was distracted of my wits,
Go kill my dearest friend, and thou hast done 't.
For let me but examine well the cause:

What was the meanness of her match to me?
Only I must confess I had a hope,
Had she continu'd widow, to have gain'd
An infinite mass of treasure by her death:
And that was the main cause,—her marriage,
That drew a stream of gall quite through my heart.
For thee, as we observe in tragedies
That a good actor many times is curs'd
For playing a villain's part, I hate thee for 't,
And, for my sake, say, thou hast done much ill well.

BOSOLA
Let me quicken your memory, for I perceive
You are falling into ingratitude: I challenge
The reward due to my service.

FERDINAND
I 'll tell thee
What I 'll give thee.

BOSOLA
Do.

FERDINAND
I 'll give thee a pardon
For this murder.

BOSOLA
Ha!

FERDINAND
Yes, and 'tis
The largest bounty I can study to do thee.
By what authority didst thou execute
This bloody sentence?

BOSOLA
By yours.

FERDINAND
Mine! was I her judge?
Did any ceremonial form of law
Doom her to not-being? Did a complete jury
Deliver her conviction up i' the court?
Where shalt thou find this judgment register'd,
Unless in hell? See, like a bloody fool,
Thou 'st forfeited thy life, and thou shalt die for 't.

BOSOLA
The office of justice is perverted quite
When one thief hangs another. Who shall dare
To reveal this?

FERDINAND
O, I 'll tell thee;
The wolf shall find her grave, and scrape it up,
Not to devour the corpse, but to discover
The horrid murder.

BOSOLA
You, not I, shall quake for 't.

FERDINAND
Leave me.

BOSOLA
I will first receive my pension.

FERDINAND
You are a villain.

BOSOLA
When your ingratitude
Is judge, I am so.

FERDINAND
O horror,
That not the fear of him which binds the devils
Can prescribe man obedience!—
Never look upon me more.

BOSOLA
Why, fare thee well.
Your brother and yourself are worthy men!
You have a pair of hearts are hollow graves,
Rotten, and rotting others; and your vengeance,
Like two chain'd-bullets, still goes arm in arm:
You may be brothers; for treason, like the plague,
Doth take much in a blood. I stand like one
That long hath ta'en a sweet and golden dream:
I am angry with myself, now that I wake.

FERDINAND
Get thee into some unknown part o' the world,
That I may never see thee.

BOSOLA
Let me know
Wherefore I should be thus neglected. Sir,
I serv'd your tyranny, and rather strove
To satisfy yourself than all the world:
And though I loath'd the evil, yet I lov'd
You that did counsel it; and rather sought
To appear a true servant than an honest man.

FERDINAND
I'll go hunt the badger by owl-light:
'Tis a deed of darkness.

[Exit.]

BOSOLA
He's much distracted. Off, my painted honour!
While with vain hopes our faculties we tire,
We seem to sweat in ice and freeze in fire.
What would I do, were this to do again?
I would not change my peace of conscience
For all the wealth of Europe.—She stirs; here's life:—
Return, fair soul, from darkness, and lead mine
Out of this sensible hell:—she's warm, she breathes:—
Upon thy pale lips I will melt my heart,
To store them with fresh colour.—Who's there?
Some cordial drink!—Alas! I dare not call:
So pity would destroy pity.—Her eye opes,
And heaven in it seems to ope, that late was shut,
To take me up to mercy.

DUCHESS
Antonio!

BOSOLA
Yes, madam, he is living;
The dead bodies you saw were but feign'd statues.
He's reconcil'd to your brothers; the Pope hath wrought
The atonement.

DUCHESS
Mercy!

[Dies.]

BOSOLA
O, she's gone again! there the cords of life broke.
O sacred innocence, that sweetly sleeps

On turtles' feathers, whilst a guilty conscience
Is a black register wherein is writ
All our good deeds and bad, a perspective
That shows us hell! That we cannot be suffer'd
To do good when we have a mind to it!
This is manly sorrow;
These tears, I am very certain, never grew
In my mother's milk. My estate is sunk
Below the degree of fear: where were
These penitent fountains while she was living?
O, they were frozen up! Here is a sight
As direful to my soul as is the sword
Unto a wretch hath slain his father.
Come, I 'll bear thee hence,
And execute thy last will; that 's deliver
Thy body to the reverend dispose
Of some good women: that the cruel tyrant
Shall not deny me. Then I 'll post to Milan,
Where somewhat I will speedily enact
Worth my dejection.

[Exit with the **BODY**].

ACT V

SCENE I [120]

[Enter **ANTONIO** and **DELIO**]

ANTONIO
What think you of my hope of reconcilement
To the Arragonian brethren?

DELIO
I misdoubt it;
For though they have sent their letters of safe-conduct
For your repair to Milan, they appear
But nets to entrap you. The Marquis of Pescara,
Under whom you hold certain land in cheat,[121]
Much 'gainst his noble nature hath been mov'd
To seize those lands; and some of his dependants
Are at this instant making it their suit
To be invested in your revenues.
I cannot think they mean well to your life
That do deprive you of your means of life,
Your living.

ANTONIO
You are still an heretic[122]
To any safety I can shape myself.

DELIO
Here comes the marquis: I will make myself
Petitioner for some part of your land,
To know whither it is flying.

ANTONIO
I pray, do.

[Withdraws.]

[Enter **PESCARA**]

DELIO
Sir, I have a suit to you.

PESCARA
To me?

DELIO
An easy one:
There is the Citadel of Saint Bennet,
With some demesnes, of late in the possession
Of Antonio Bologna,—please you bestow them on me.

PESCARA
You are my friend; but this is such a suit,
Nor fit for me to give, nor you to take.

DELIO
No, sir?

PESCARA
I will give you ample reason for 't
Soon in private:—here 's the cardinal's mistress.

[Enter **JULIA**]

JULIA
My lord, I am grown your poor petitioner,
And should be an ill beggar, had I not
A great man's letter here, the cardinal's,
To court you in my favour.

[Gives a letter.]

PESCARA
He entreats for you
The Citadel of Saint Bennet, that belong'd
To the banish'd Bologna.

JULIA
Yes.

PESCARA
I could not have thought of a friend I could rather
Pleasure with it: 'tis yours.

JULIA
Sir, I thank you;
And he shall know how doubly I am engag'd
Both in your gift, and speediness of giving
Which makes your grant the greater.

[Exit.]

ANTONIO
How they fortify
Themselves with my ruin!

DELIO
Sir, I am
Little bound to you.

PESCARA
Why?

DELIO
Because you deni'd this suit to me, and gave 't
To such a creature.

PESCARA
Do you know what it was?
It was Antonio's land; not forfeited
By course of law, but ravish'd from his throat
By the cardinal's entreaty. It were not fit
I should bestow so main a piece of wrong
Upon my friend; 'tis a gratification
Only due to a strumpet, for it is injustice.
Shall I sprinkle the pure blood of innocents
To make those followers I call my friends
Look ruddier upon me? I am glad

This land, ta'en from the owner by such wrong,
Returns again unto so foul an use
As salary for his lust. Learn, good Delio,
To ask noble things of me, and you shall find
I 'll be a noble giver.

DELIO
You instruct me well.

ANTONIO
Why, here 's a man now would fright impudence
From sauciest beggars.

PESCARA
Prince Ferdinand 's come to Milan,
Sick, as they give out, of an apoplexy;
But some say 'tis a frenzy: I am going
To visit him.

[Exit.]

ANTONIO
'Tis a noble old fellow.

DELIO
What course do you mean to take, Antonio?

ANTONIO
This night I mean to venture all my fortune,
Which is no more than a poor ling'ring life,
To the cardinal's worst of malice. I have got
Private access to his chamber; and intend
To visit him about the mid of night,
As once his brother did our noble duchess.
It may be that the sudden apprehension
Of danger,—for I 'll go in mine own shape,—
When he shall see it fraight[123] with love and duty,
May draw the poison out of him, and work
A friendly reconcilement. If it fail,
Yet it shall rid me of this infamous calling;
For better fall once than be ever falling.

DELIO
I 'll second you in all danger; and howe'er,
My life keeps rank with yours.

ANTONIO
You are still my lov'd and best friend.

[Exeunt.]

SCENE II[124]

[Enter **PESCARA** and **DOCTOR**.

PESCARA
Now, doctor, may I visit your patient?

DOCTOR
If 't please your lordship; but he 's instantly
To take the air here in the gallery
By my direction.

PESCARA
Pray thee, what 's his disease?

DOCTOR
A very pestilent disease, my lord,
They call lycanthropia.

PESCARA
What 's that?
I need a dictionary to 't.

DOCTOR
I 'll tell you.
In those that are possess'd with 't there o'erflows
Such melancholy humour they imagine
Themselves to be transformed into wolves;
Steal forth to church-yards in the dead of night,
And dig dead bodies up: as two nights since
One met the duke 'bout midnight in a lane
Behind Saint Mark's church, with the leg of a man
Upon his shoulder; and he howl'd fearfully;
Said he was a wolf, only the difference
Was, a wolf's skin was hairy on the outside,
His on the inside; bade them take their swords,
Rip up his flesh, and try. Straight I was sent for,
And, having minister'd to him, found his grace
Very well recover'd.

PESCARA
I am glad on 't.

DOCTOR
Yet not without some fear
Of a relapse
If he grow to his fit again,
I 'll go a nearer way to work with him
Than ever Paracelsus dream'd of; if
They 'll give me leave, I 'll buffet his madness out of him.
Stand aside; he comes.

[Enter **FERDINAND**, **CARDINAL**, **MALATESTI**, and **BOSOLA**]

FERDINAND
Leave me.

MALATESTI
Why doth your lordship love this solitariness?

FERDINAND
Eagles commonly fly alone: they are crows, daws, and starlings that flock together
Look, what 's that follows me?

MALATESTI
Nothing, my lord.

FERDINAND
Yes.

MALATESTI
'Tis your shadow.

FERDINAND
Stay it; let it not haunt me.

MALATESTI
Impossible, if you move, and the sun shine.

FERDINAND
I will throttle it.

[Throws himself down on his shadow.]

MALATESTI
O, my lord, you are angry with nothing.

FERDINAND
You are a fool: how is 't possible I should catch my shadow, unless I fall upon 't? When I go to hell, I mean to carry a bribe; for, look you, good gifts evermore make way for the worst persons.

PESCARA
Rise, good my lord.

FERDINAND
I am studying the art of patience.

PESCARA
'Tis a noble virtue.

FERDINAND
To drive six snails before me from this town to Moscow; neither use goad nor whip to them, but let them take their own time; —the patient'st man i' th' world match me for an experiment:—an I 'll crawl after like a sheep-biter.[125]

CARDINAL
Force him up.

[They raise him.]

FERDINAND
Use me well, you were best
What I have done, I have done:
I 'll confess nothing.

DOCTOR
Now let me come to him.—Are you mad, my lord? are you out of your princely wits?

FERDINAND
What 's he?

PESCARA
Your doctor.

FERDINAND
Let me have his beard saw'd off, and his eye-brows fil'd more civil.

DOCTOR
I must do mad tricks with him, for that 's the only way on 't.—I have brought your grace a salamander's skin to keep you from sun-burning.

FERDINAND
I have cruel sore eyes.

DOCTOR
The white of a cockatrix's[126] egg is present remedy.

FERDINAND
Let it be a new-laid one, you were best.

Hide me from him: physicians are like kings,—
They brook no contradiction.

DOCTOR
Now he begins to fear me: now let me alone with him.

CARDINAL
How now! put off your gown!

DOCTOR
Let me have some forty urinals filled with rosewater: he and I 'll go pelt one another with them.—Now he begins to fear me.—Can you fetch a frisk,[127] sir?—Let him go, let him go, upon my peril: I find by his eye he stands in awe of me; I 'll make him as tame as a dormouse.

FERDINAND
Can you fetch your frisks, sir!—I will stamp him into a cullis,[128] flay off his skin to cover one of the anatomies[129] this rogue hath set i' th' cold yonder in Barber-Chirurgeon's-hall.—Hence, hence! you are all of you like beasts for sacrifice.

[Throws the **DOCTOR** down and beats him.]

There 's nothing left of you but tongue and belly, flattery and lechery.

[Exit.]

PESCARA
Doctor, he did not fear you thoroughly.

DOCTOR
True; I was somewhat too forward.

BOSOLA
Mercy upon me, what a fatal judgment
Hath fall'n upon this Ferdinand!

PESCARA
Knows your grace
What accident hath brought unto the prince
This strange distraction?

CARDINAL [Aside.]
I must feign somewhat.—Thus they say it grew.
You have heard it rumour'd, for these many years
None of our family dies but there is seen
The shape of an old woman, which is given
By tradition to us to have been murder'd
By her nephews for her riches. Such a figure
One night, as the prince sat up late at 's book,

Appear'd to him; when crying out for help,
The gentleman of 's chamber found his grace
All on a cold sweat, alter'd much in face
And language: since which apparition,
He hath grown worse and worse, and I much fear
He cannot live.

BOSOLA
Sir, I would speak with you.

PESCARA
We 'll leave your grace,
Wishing to the sick prince, our noble lord,
All health of mind and body.

CARDINAL
You are most welcome.

[Exeunt **PESCARA**, **MALATESTI**, and **DOCTOR**.]

Are you come? so.—[Aside.] This fellow must not know
By any means I had intelligence
In our duchess' death; for, though I counsell'd it,
The full of all th' engagement seem'd to grow
From Ferdinand.—Now, sir, how fares our sister?
I do not think but sorrow makes her look
Like to an oft-dy'd garment: she shall now
Take comfort from me. Why do you look so wildly?
O, the fortune of your master here the prince
Dejects you; but be you of happy comfort:
If you 'll do one thing for me I 'll entreat,
Though he had a cold tomb-stone o'er his bones,
I 'd make you what you would be.

BOSOLA
Any thing;
Give it me in a breath, and let me fly to 't.
They that think long small expedition win,
For musing much o' th' end cannot begin.

[Enter **JULIA**]

JULIA
Sir, will you come into supper?

CARDINAL
I am busy; leave me.

JULIA [Aside.]
What an excellent shape hath that fellow!

[Exit.

CARDINAL
'Tis thus. Antonio lurks here in Milan:
Inquire him out, and kill him. While he lives,
Our sister cannot marry; and I have thought
Of an excellent match for her. Do this, and style me
Thy advancement.

BOSOLA
But by what means shall I find him out?

CARDINAL
There is a gentleman call'd Delio
Here in the camp, that hath been long approv'd
His loyal friend. Set eye upon that fellow;
Follow him to mass; may be Antonio,
Although he do account religion
But a school-name, for fashion of the world
May accompany him; or else go inquire out
Delio's confessor, and see if you can bribe
Him to reveal it. There are a thousand ways
A man might find to trace him; as to know
What fellows haunt the Jews for taking up
Great sums of money, for sure he 's in want;
Or else to go to the picture-makers, and learn
Who bought[130] her picture lately: some of these
Happily may take.

BOSOLA
Well, I 'll not freeze i' th' business:
I would see that wretched thing, Antonio,
Above all sights i' th' world.

CARDINAL
Do, and be happy.

[Exit.]

BOSOLA
This fellow doth breed basilisks in 's eyes,
He 's nothing else but murder; yet he seems
Not to have notice of the duchess' death.
'Tis his cunning: I must follow his example;
There cannot be a surer way to trace

Than that of an old fox.

[Re-enter **JULIA**, with a pistol]

JULIA
So, sir, you are well met.

BOSOLA
How Now!

JULIA
Nay, the doors are fast enough:
Now, sir, I will make you confess your treachery.

BOSOLA
Treachery!

JULIA
Yes, confess to me
Which of my women 'twas you hir'd to put
Love-powder into my drink?

BOSOLA
Love-powder!

JULIA
Yes, when I was at Malfi.
Why should I fall in love with such a face else?
I have already suffer'd for thee so much pain,
The only remedy to do me good
Is to kill my longing.

BOSOLA
Sure, your pistol holds
Nothing but perfumes or kissing-comfits.[131]
Excellent lady!
You have a pretty way on 't to discover
Your longing. Come, come, I 'll disarm you,
And arm you thus: yet this is wondrous strange.

JULIA
Compare thy form and my eyes together,
You 'll find my love no such great miracle.
Now you 'll say
I am wanton: this nice modesty in ladies
Is but a troublesome familiar
That haunts them.

BOSOLA
Know you me, I am a blunt soldier.

JULIA
The better:
Sure, there wants fire where there are no lively sparks
Of roughness.

BOSOLA
And I want compliment.

JULIA
Why, ignorance
In courtship cannot make you do amiss,
If you have a heart to do well.

BOSOLA
You are very fair.

JULIA
Nay, if you lay beauty to my charge,
I must plead unguilty.

BOSOLA
Your bright eyes
Carry a quiver of darts in them sharper
Than sun-beams.

JULIA
You will mar me with commendation,
Put yourself to the charge of courting me,
Whereas now I woo you.

BOSOLA [Aside.]
I have it, I will work upon this creature.—
Let us grow most amorously familiar:
If the great cardinal now should see me thus,
Would he not count me a villain?

JULIA
No; he might count me a wanton,
Not lay a scruple of offence on you;
For if I see and steal a diamond,
The fault is not i' th' stone, but in me the thief
That purloins it. I am sudden with you.
We that are great women of pleasure use to cut off
These uncertain wishes and unquiet longings,
And in an instant join the sweet delight

And the pretty excuse together. Had you been i' th' street,
Under my chamber-window, even there
I should have courted you.

BOSOLA
O, you are an excellent lady!

JULIA
Bid me do somewhat for you presently
To express I love you.

BOSOLA
I will; and if you love me,
Fail not to effect it.
The cardinal is grown wondrous melancholy;
Demand the cause, let him not put you off
With feign'd excuse; discover the main ground on 't.

JULIA
Why would you know this?

BOSOLA
I have depended on him,
And I hear that he is fall'n in some disgrace
With the emperor: if he be, like the mice
That forsake falling houses, I would shift
To other dependance.

JULIA
You shall not need
Follow the wars: I 'll be your maintenance.

BOSOLA
And I your loyal servant: but I cannot
Leave my calling.

JULIA
Not leave an ungrateful
General for the love of a sweet lady!
You are like some cannot sleep in feather-beds,
But must have blocks for their pillows.

BOSOLA
Will you do this?

JULIA
Cunningly.

BOSOLA
To-morrow I'll expect th' intelligence.

JULIA
To-morrow! get you into my cabinet;
You shall have it with you. Do not delay me,
No more than I do you: I am like one
That is condemn'd; I have my pardon promis'd,
But I would see it seal'd. Go, get you in:
You shall see my wind my tongue about his heart
Like a skein of silk.

[Exit BOSOLA]

[Re-enter CARDINAL]

CARDINAL
Where are you?

[Enter SERVANTS.]

SERVANTS
Here.

CARDINAL
Let none, upon your lives, have conference
With the Prince Ferdinand, unless I know it.—
[Aside] In this distraction he may reveal
The murder.

[Exeunt SERVANTS.]

Yond's my lingering consumption:
I am weary of her, and by any means
Would be quit of.

JULIA
How now, my lord! what ails you?

CARDINAL
Nothing.

JULIA
O, you are much alter'd:
Come, I must be your secretary, and remove
This lead from off your bosom: what's the matter?

CARDINAL

I may not tell you.

JULIA
Are you so far in love with sorrow
You cannot part with part of it? Or think you
I cannot love your grace when you are sad
As well as merry? Or do you suspect
I, that have been a secret to your heart
These many winters, cannot be the same
Unto your tongue?

CARDINAL
Satisfy thy longing,—
The only way to make thee keep my counsel
Is, not to tell thee.

JULIA
Tell your echo this,
Or flatterers, that like echoes still report
What they hear though most imperfect, and not me;
For if that you be true unto yourself,
I 'll know.

CARDINAL
Will you rack me?

JULIA
No, judgment shall
Draw it from you: it is an equal fault,
To tell one's secrets unto all or none.

CARDINAL
The first argues folly.

JULIA
But the last tyranny.

CARDINAL
Very well: why, imagine I have committed
Some secret deed which I desire the world
May never hear of.

JULIA
Therefore may not I know it?
You have conceal'd for me as great a sin
As adultery. Sir, never was occasion
For perfect trial of my constancy
Till now: sir, I beseech you—

CARDINAL
You 'll repent it.

JULIA
Never.

CARDINAL
It hurries thee to ruin: I 'll not tell thee.
Be well advis'd, and think what danger 'tis
To receive a prince's secrets. They that do,
Had need have their breasts hoop'd with adamant
To contain them. I pray thee, yet be satisfi'd;
Examine thine own frailty; 'tis more easy
To tie knots than unloose them. 'Tis a secret
That, like a ling'ring poison, may chance lie
Spread in thy veins, and kill thee seven year hence.

JULIA
Now you dally with me.

CARDINAL
No more; thou shalt know it.
By my appointment the great Duchess of Malfi
And two of her young children, four nights since,
Were strangl'd.

JULIA
O heaven! sir, what have you done!

CARDINAL
How now? How settles this? Think you your bosom
Will be a grave dark and obscure enough
For such a secret?

JULIA
You have undone yourself, sir.

CARDINAL
Why?

JULIA
It lies not in me to conceal it.

CARDINAL
No?
Come, I will swear you to 't upon this book.

JULIA
Most religiously.

CARDINAL
Kiss it.

[She kisses the book.]

Now you shall never utter it; thy curiosity
Hath undone thee; thou 'rt poison'd with that book.
Because I knew thou couldst not keep my counsel,
I have bound thee to 't by death.

[Re-enter **BOSOLA**]

BOSOLA
For pity-sake, hold!

CARDINAL
Ha, Bosola!

JULIA
I forgive you
This equal piece of justice you have done;
For I betray'd your counsel to that fellow.
He over-heard it; that was the cause I said
It lay not in me to conceal it.

BOSOLA
O foolish woman,
Couldst not thou have poison'd him?

JULIA
'Tis weakness,
Too much to think what should have been done. I go,
I know not whither.

[Dies.]

CARDINAL
Wherefore com'st thou hither?

BOSOLA
That I might find a great man like yourself,
Not out of his wits, as the Lord Ferdinand,
To remember my service.

CARDINAL

I'll have thee hew'd in pieces.

BOSOLA
Make not yourself such a promise of that life
Which is not yours to dispose of.

CARDINAL
Who plac'd thee here?

BOSOLA
Her lust, as she intended.

CARDINAL
Very well:
Now you know me for your fellow-murderer.

BOSOLA
And wherefore should you lay fair marble colours
Upon your rotten purposes to me?
Unless you imitate some that do plot great treasons,
And when they have done, go hide themselves i' th' grave
Of those were actors in 't?

CARDINAL
No more; there is
A fortune attends thee.

BOSOLA
Shall I go sue to Fortune any longer?
'Tis the fool's pilgrimage.

CARDINAL
I have honours in store for thee.

BOSOLA
There are a many ways that conduct to seeming
Honour, and some of them very dirty ones.

CARDINAL
Throw to the devil
Thy melancholy. The fire burns well;
What need we keep a stirring of 't, and make
A greater smother?[132] Thou wilt kill Antonio?

BOSOLA
Yes.

CARDINAL

Take up that body.

BOSOLA
I think I shall
Shortly grow the common bier for church-yards.

CARDINAL
I will allow thee some dozen of attendants
To aid thee in the murder.

BOSOLA
O, by no means. Physicians that apply horse-leeches to any rank swelling use to cut off their tails, that the blood may run through them the faster: let me have no train when I go to shed blood, less it make me have a greater when I ride to the gallows.

CARDINAL
Come to me after midnight, to help to remove
That body to her own lodging. I'll give out
She died o' th' plague; 'twill breed the less inquiry
After her death.

BOSOLA
Where's Castruccio her husband?

CARDINAL
He's rode to Naples, to take possession
Of Antonio's citadel.

BOSOLA
Believe me, you have done a very happy turn.

CARDINAL
Fail not to come. There is the master-key
Of our lodgings; and by that you may conceive
What trust I plant in you.

BOSOLA
You shall find me ready.

[Exit **CARDINAL**.

O poor Antonio, though nothing be so needful
To thy estate as pity, yet I find
Nothing so dangerous! I must look to my footing:
In such slippery ice-pavements men had need
To be frost-nail'd well, they may break their necks else;
The precedent's here afore me. How this man
Bears up in blood! seems fearless! Why, 'tis well;

Security some men call the suburbs of hell,
Only a dead wall between. Well, good Antonio,
I 'll seek thee out; and all my care shall be
To put thee into safety from the reach
Of these most cruel biters that have got
Some of thy blood already. It may be,
I 'll join with thee in a most just revenge.
The weakest arm is strong enough that strikes
With the sword of justice. Still methinks the duchess
Haunts me: there, there!—'Tis nothing but my melancholy.
O Penitence, let me truly taste thy cup,
That throws men down only to raise them up!

Exit.

SCENE III [133]

[Enter **ANTONIO** and **DELIO**

ECHO from the **DUCHESS'S** Grave)

DELIO
Yond 's the cardinal's window. This fortification
Grew from the ruins of an ancient abbey;
And to yond side o' th' river lies a wall,
Piece of a cloister, which in my opinion
Gives the best echo that you ever heard,
So hollow and so dismal, and withal
So plain in the distinction of our words,
That many have suppos'd it is a spirit
That answers.

ANTONIO
I do love these ancient ruins.
We never tread upon them but we set
Our foot upon some reverend history;
And, questionless, here in this open court,
Which now lies naked to the injuries
Of stormy weather, some men lie interr'd
Lov'd the church so well, and gave so largely to 't,
They thought it should have canopied their bones
Till dooms-day. But all things have their end;
Churches and cities, which have diseases like to men,
Must have like death that we have.

ECHO

Like death that we have.

DELIO
Now the echo hath caught you.

ANTONIO
It groan'd methought, and gave
A very deadly accent.

ECHO
Deadly accent.

DELIO
I told you 'twas a pretty one. You may make it
A huntsman, or a falconer, a musician,
Or a thing of sorrow.

ECHO
A thing of sorrow.

ANTONIO
Ay, sure, that suits it best.

ECHO
That suits it best.

ANTONIO
'Tis very like my wife's voice.

ECHO
Ay, wife's voice.

DELIO
Come, let us walk further from t.
I would not have you go to the cardinal's to-night:
Do not.

ECHO
Do not.

DELIO
Wisdom doth not more moderate wasting sorrow
Than time. Take time for 't; be mindful of thy safety.

ECHO
Be mindful of thy safety.

ANTONIO

Necessity compels me.
Make scrutiny through the passages
Of your own life, you 'll find it impossible
To fly your fate.

ECHO
O, fly your fate!

DELIO
Hark! the dead stones seem to have pity on you,
And give you good counsel.

ANTONIO
Echo, I will not talk with thee,
For thou art a dead thing.

ECHO
Thou art a dead thing.

ANTONIO
My duchess is asleep now,
And her little ones, I hope sweetly. O heaven,
Shall I never see her more?

ECHO
Never see her more.

ANTONIO
I mark'd not one repetition of the echo
But that; and on the sudden a clear light
Presented me a face folded in sorrow.

DELIO
Your fancy merely.

ANTONIO
Come, I 'll be out of this ague,
For to live thus is not indeed to live;
It is a mockery and abuse of life.
I will not henceforth save myself by halves;
Lose all, or nothing.

DELIO
Your own virtue save you!
I 'll fetch your eldest son, and second you.
It may be that the sight of his own blood
Spread in so sweet a figure may beget
The more compassion. However, fare you well.

Though in our miseries Fortune have a part,
Yet in our noble sufferings she hath none.
Contempt of pain, that we may call our own.

[Exeunt.]

SCENE IV [134]

[Enter **CARDINAL, PESCARA, MALATESTI, RODERIGO,** and **GRISOLAN**]

CARDINAL
You shall not watch to-night by the sick prince;
His grace is very well recover'd.

MALATESTI
Good my lord, suffer us.

CARDINAL
O, by no means;
The noise, and change of object in his eye,
Doth more distract him. I pray, all to bed;
And though you hear him in his violent fit,
Do not rise, I entreat you.

PESCARA
So, sir; we shall not.

CARDINAL
Nay, I must have you promise
Upon your honours, for I was enjoin'd to 't
By himself; and he seem'd to urge it sensibly.

PESCARA
Let our honours bind this trifle.

CARDINAL
Nor any of your followers.

MALATESTI
Neither.

CARDINAL
It may be, to make trial of your promise,
When he 's asleep, myself will rise and feign
Some of his mad tricks, and cry out for help,
And feign myself in danger.

MALATESTI
If your throat were cutting,
I 'd not come at you, now I have protested against it.

CARDINAL
Why, I thank you.

GRISOLAN
'Twas a foul storm to-night.

RODERIGO
The Lord Ferdinand's chamber shook like an osier.

MALATESTI
'Twas nothing put pure kindness in the devil
To rock his own child.

[Exeunt all except the **CARDINAL**].

CARDINAL
The reason why I would not suffer these
About my brother, is, because at midnight
I may with better privacy convey
Julia's body to her own lodging. O, my conscience!
I would pray now; but the devil takes away my heart
For having any confidence in prayer.
About this hour I appointed Bosola
To fetch the body. When he hath serv'd my turn,
He dies.

[Exit.]

[Enter **BOSOLA**]

BOSOLA
Ha! 'twas the cardinal's voice; I heard him name
Bosola and my death. Listen; I hear one's footing.

[Enter **FERDINAND**]

FERDINAND
Strangling is a very quiet death.

BOSOLA [Aside.]
Nay, then, I see I must stand upon my guard.

FERDINAND

What say to that? Whisper softly: do you agree to 't?
So; it must be done i' th' dark; the cardinal would not for
A thousand pounds the doctor should see it.

[Exit.]

BOSOLA
My death is plotted; here 's the consequence of murder.
We value not desert nor Christian breath,
When we know black deeds must be cur'd with death.

[Enter **ANTONIO** and **SERVANT**]

SERVANT
Here stay, sir, and be confident, I pray;
I 'll fetch you a dark lantern.

[Exit.]

ANTONIO
Could I take him at his prayers,
There were hope of pardon.

BOSOLA
Fall right, my sword!—

[Stabs him.]

I 'll not give thee so much leisure as to pray.

ANTONIO
O, I am gone! Thou hast ended a long suit
In a minute.

BOSOLA
What art thou?

ANTONIO
A most wretched thing,
That only have thy benefit in death,
To appear myself.

[Re-enter **SERVANT** with a lantern]

SERVANT
Where are you, sir?

ANTONIO

Very near my home.—Bosola!

SERVANT
O, misfortune!

BOSOLA
Smother thy pity, thou art dead else.—Antonio!
The man I would have sav'd 'bove mine own life!
We are merely the stars' tennis-balls, struck and banded
Which way please them.—O good Antonio,
I 'll whisper one thing in thy dying ear
Shall make thy heart break quickly! Thy fair duchess
And two sweet children—

ANTONIO
Their very names
Kindle a little life in me.

BOSOLA
Are murder'd.

ANTONIO
Some men have wish'd to die
At the hearing of sad tidings; I am glad
That I shall do 't in sadness.[135] I would not now
Wish my wounds balm'd nor heal'd, for I have no use
To put my life to. In all our quest of greatness,
Like wanton boys whose pastime is their care,
We follow after bubbles blown in th' air.
Pleasure of life, what is 't? Only the good hours
Of an ague; merely a preparative to rest,
To endure vexation. I do not ask
The process of my death; only commend me
To Delio.

BOSOLA
Break, heart!

ANTONIO
And let my son fly the courts to princes.

[Dies.]

BOSOLA
Thou seem'st to have lov'd Antonio.

SERVANT
I brought him hither,

To have reconcil'd him to the cardinal.

BOSOLA
I do not ask thee that.
Take him up, if thou tender thine own life,
And bear him where the lady Julia
Was wont to lodge.—O, my fate moves swift!
I have this cardinal in the forge already;
Now I 'll bring him to th' hammer. O direful misprision![136]
I will not imitate things glorious.
No more than base; I 'll be mine own example.—
On, on, and look thou represent, for silence,
The thing thou bear'st.[137]

[Exeunt.]

SCENE V [138]

[Enter **CARDINAL**, with a book

CARDINAL
I am puzzl'd in a question about hell;
He says, in hell there 's one material fire,
And yet it shall not burn all men alike.
Lay him by. How tedious is a guilty conscience!
When I look into the fish-ponds in my garden,
Methinks I see a thing arm'd with a rake,
That seems to strike at me.

[Enter **BOSOLA**, and **SERVANT** bearing **ANTONIO'S** body]

Now, art thou come?
Thou look'st ghastly;
There sits in thy face some great determination
Mix'd with some fear.

BOSOLA
Thus it lightens into action:
I am come to kill thee.

CARDINAL
Ha!—Help! our guard!

BOSOLA
Thou art deceiv'd; they are out of thy howling.

CARDINAL
Hold; and I will faithfully divide
Revenues with thee.

BOSOLA
Thy prayers and proffers
Are both unseasonable.

CARDINAL
Raise the watch!
We are betray'd!

BOSOLA
I have confin'd your flight:
I 'll suffer your retreat to Julia's chamber,
But no further.

CARDINAL
Help! we are betray'd!

[Enter, above, **PESCARA**, **MALATESTI**, **RODERIGO**, and **GRISOLAN**]

MALATESTI
Listen.

CARDINAL
My dukedom for rescue!

RODERIGO
Fie upon his counterfeiting!

MALATESTI
Why, 'tis not the cardinal.

RODERIGO
Yes, yes, 'tis he:
But, I 'll see him hang'd ere I 'll go down to him.

CARDINAL
Here 's a plot upon me; I am assaulted! I am lost,
Unless some rescue!

GRISOLAN
He doth this pretty well;
But it will not serve to laugh me out of mine honour.

CARDINAL
The sword's at my throat!

RODERIGO
You would not bawl so loud then.

MALATESTI
Come, come, let 's go to bed: he told us this much aforehand.

PESCARA
He wish'd you should not come at him; but, believe 't,
The accent of the voice sounds not in jest:
I 'll down to him, howsoever, and with engines
Force ope the doors.

[Exit above.]

RODERIGO
Let 's follow him aloof,
And note how the cardinal will laugh at him.

[Exeunt, above, **MALATESTI**, **RODERIGO**, and **GRISOLAN**.]

BOSOLA
There 's for you first,
'Cause you shall not unbarricade the door
To let in rescue.

[Kills the **SERVANT**.]

CARDINAL
What cause hast thou to pursue my life?

BOSOLA
Look there.

CARDINAL
Antonio!

BOSOLA
Slain by my hand unwittingly.
Pray, and be sudden
When thou kill'd'st thy sister,
Thou took'st from Justice her most equal balance,
And left her naught but her sword.

CARDINAL
O, mercy!

BOSOLA

Now it seems thy greatness was only outward;
For thou fall'st faster of thyself than calamity
Can drive thee. I'll not waste longer time; there!

[Stabs him.]

CARDINAL
Thou hast hurt me.

BOSOLA
Again!

CARDINAL
Shall I die like a leveret,
Without any resistance?—Help, help, help!
I am slain!

[Enter **FERDINAND**]

FERDINAND
Th' alarum! Give me a fresh horse;
Rally the vaunt-guard, or the day is lost,
Yield, yield! I give you the honour of arms
Shake my sword over you; will you yield?

CARDINAL
Help me; I am your brother!

FERDINAND
The devil!
My brother fight upon the adverse party!

[He wounds the **CARDINAL**, and, in the scuffle, gives **BOSOLA** his death-wound.]

There flies your ransom.

CARDINAL
O justice!
I suffer now for what hath former bin:
Sorrow is held the eldest child of sin.

FERDINAND
Now you're brave fellows. Caesar's fortune was harder than Pompey's; Caesar died in the arms of prosperity, Pompey at the feet of disgrace. You both died in the field. The pain's nothing; pain many times is taken away with the apprehension of greater, as the tooth-ache with the sight of a barber that comes to pull it out. There's philosophy for you.

BOSOLA

Now my revenge is perfect.—Sink, thou main cause

[Kills **FERDINAND**.]

Of my undoing!—The last part of my life
Hath done me best service.

FERDINAND
Give me some wet hay; I am broken-winded.
I do account this world but a dog-kennel:
I will vault credit and affect high pleasures
Beyond death.

BOSOLA
He seems to come to himself,
Now he 's so near the bottom.

FERDINAND
My sister, O my sister! there 's the cause on 't.
Whether we fall by ambition, blood, or lust,
Like diamonds, we are cut with our own dust.

[Dies.]

CARDINAL
Thou hast thy payment too.

BOSOLA
Yes, I hold my weary soul in my teeth;
'Tis ready to part from me. I do glory
That thou, which stood'st like a huge pyramid
Begun upon a large and ample base,
Shalt end in a little point, a kind of nothing.

[Enter, below, **PESCARA**, **MALATESTI**, **RODERIGO**, and **GRISOLAN**]

PESCARA
How now, my lord!

MALATESTI
O sad disaster!

RODERIGO
How comes this?

BOSOLA
Revenge for the Duchess of Malfi murdered
By the Arragonian brethren; for Antonio

Slain by this hand; for lustful Julia
Poison'd by this man; and lastly for myself,
That was an actor in the main of all
Much 'gainst mine own good nature, yet i' the end
Neglected.

PESCARA
How now, my lord!

CARDINAL
Look to my brother:
He gave us these large wounds, as we were struggling
Here i' th' rushes. And now, I pray, let me
Be laid by and never thought of.

[Dies.]

PESCARA
How fatally, it seems, he did withstand
His own rescue!

MALATESTI
Thou wretched thing of blood,
How came Antonio by his death?

BOSOLA
In a mist; I know not how:
Such a mistake as I have often seen
In a play. O, I am gone!
We are only like dead walls or vaulted graves,
That, ruin'd, yield no echo. Fare you well.
It may be pain, but no harm, to me to die
In so good a quarrel. O, this gloomy world!
In what a shadow, or deep pit of darkness,
Doth womanish and fearful mankind live!
Let worthy minds ne'er stagger in distrust
To suffer death or shame for what is just:
Mine is another voyage.

[Dies.]

PESCARA
The noble Delio, as I came to th' palace,
Told me of Antonio's being here, and show'd me
A pretty gentleman, his son and heir.

[Enter **DELIO**, and **ANTONIO'S SON**]

MALATESTI
O sir, you come too late!

DELIO
I heard so, and
Was arm'd for 't, ere I came
Let us make noble use
Of this great ruin; and join all our force
To establish this young hopeful gentleman
In 's mother's right
These wretched eminent things
Leave no more fame behind 'em, than should one
Fall in a frost, and leave his print in snow;
As soon as the sun shines, it ever melts,
Both form and matter
I have ever thought
Nature doth nothing so great for great men
As when she 's pleas'd to make them lords of truth:
Integrity of life is fame's best friend,
Which nobly, beyond death, shall crown the end.

[Exeunt.]

FOOTNOTES:

[Footnote 1: Malfi. The presence-chamber in the palace of the Duchess.]

[Footnote 2: Prevent.]

[Footnote 3: The same.]

[Footnote 4: The reference is to the knightly sport of riding at the ring.]

[Footnote 5: At the expense of.]

[Footnote 6: Rolls of lint used to dress wounds.]

[Footnote 7: Surgeons.]

[Footnote 8: A small horse.]

[Footnote 9: Ballasted.]

[Footnote 10: A lively dance.]

[Footnote 11: Throws into the shade.]

[Footnote 12: At the point of.]

[Footnote 13: Coaches.]

[Footnote 14: Spy.]

[Footnote 15: Cheats.]

[Footnote 16: Spy.]

[Footnote 17: Malfi. Gallery in the Duchess' palace.]

[Footnote 18: Lustful.]

[Footnote 19: Genesis xxxi., 31-42.]

[Footnote 20: The net in which he caught Venus and Mars.]

[Footnote 21: Housekeepers.]

[Footnote 22: Produced.]

[Footnote 23: Qq. read STRANGE.]

[Footnote 24: Guess.]

[Footnote 25: The phrase used to indicate that accounts had been examined and found correct.]

[Footnote 26: Using words of present time; i.e., "I take," not "I will take."]

[Footnote 27: Knot.]

[Footnote 28: More firmly.]

[Footnote 29: Of difficult disposition.]

[Footnote 30: Malfi. An apartment in the palace of the Duchess.]

[Footnote 31: Chief part.]

[Footnote 32: Bullies (Hazlitt); lawyers (Vaughan).]

[Footnote 33: Royal journey.]

[Footnote 34: Turning a boat on its side for repairs.]

[Footnote 35: Scabbed.]

[Footnote 36: Empty.]

[Footnote 37: Face-modeling (Sampson). "There's a plain statement of your practises."]

[Footnote 38: Blue like those of a woman with child.]

[Footnote 39: Scurf.]

[Footnote 40: Person of highest influence.]

[Footnote 41: Hysteria.]

[Footnote 42: This year.]

[Footnote 43: Clearly.]

[Footnote 44: Youngster.]

[Footnote 45: A hall in the same palace.]

[Footnote 46: Crossness.]

[Footnote 47: Always.]

[Footnote 48: The meaner servants.]

[Footnote 49: At once.]

[Footnote 50: Cast his horoscope.]

[Footnote 51: The court of the same palace.]

[Footnote 52: Making an astrological calculation.]

[Footnote 53: Going to the root of the matter.]

[Footnote 54: Write.]

[Footnote 55: i.e., on his handkerchief.]

[Footnote 56: Addressing the lantern.]

[Footnote 57: "The rest not considered."]

[Footnote 58: A piece of news.]

[Footnote 59: Cleverly contrived.]

[Footnote 60: Rome. An apartment in the palace of the Cardinal.]

[Footnote 61: Religious recluse.]

[Footnote 62: Experienced.]

[Footnote 63: Sick.]

[Footnote 64: Medicinal.]

[Footnote 65: Strong broth.]

[Footnote 66: Another apartment in the same palace.]

[Footnote 67: The mandrake was supposed to give forth shrieks when uprooted, which drove the hearer mad.]

[Footnote 68: Unchaste.]

[Footnote 69: Supposed to be a sign of folly.]

[Footnote 70: Throw the hammer.]

[Footnote 71: Boil to shreds. (Dyce.) Qq, TO BOIL.]

[Footnote 72: Malfi. An apartment in the palace of the Duchess.]

[Footnote 73: Wealth.]

[Footnote 74: Lampoons.]

[Footnote 75: Plowshares.]

[Footnote 76: Spying.]

[Footnote 77: Deceptions.]

[Footnote 78: Soothing.]

[Footnote 79: The bed-chamber of the Duchess in the same.]

[Footnote 80: Qq. read SLIGHT.]

[Footnote 81: Powder of orris-root.]

[Footnote 82: Wheels of craft.]

[Footnote 83: Certificate that the books were found correct.]

[Footnote 84: The badge of a steward.]

[Footnote 85: Spies.]

[Footnote 86: Lot.]

[Footnote 87: For Plutus.]

[Footnote 88: Quick steps.]

[Footnote 89: Miss.]

[Footnote 90: Remains.]

[Footnote 91: Profession.]

[Footnote 92: An apartment in the Cardinal's palace at Rome.]

[Footnote 93: A decorated horse-cloth, used only when the court is traveling.]

[Footnote 94: The first quarto has in the margin: "The Author disclaims this Ditty to be his."]

[Footnote 95: Near Loretto.]

[Footnote 96: Small birds.]

[Footnote 97: His vizard.]

[Footnote 98: Malfi. An apartment in the palace of the Duchess.]

[Footnote 99: Curtain.]

[Footnote 100: The wife of Brutus, who died by swallowing fire.]

[Footnote 101: By artificial means.]

[Footnote 102: Profession.]

[Footnote 103: Spying.]

[Footnote 104: Another room in the lodging of the Duchess.]

[Footnote 105: Band.]

[Footnote 106: Bands.]

[Footnote 107: Boil.]

[Footnote 108: Punning on the two senses of "dye" and "corn."]

[Footnote 109: From exporting his grain.]

[Footnote 110: Optical glass.]

[Footnote 111: The Geneva Bible.]

[Footnote 112: Petticoat.]

[Footnote 113: Coach.]

[Footnote 114: A warm drink containing milk, wine, etc.]

[Footnote 115: Receptacle.]

[Footnote 116: A drug supposed to ooze from embalmed bodies.]

[Footnote 117: Curdled.]

[Footnote 118: Trial.]

[Footnote 119: An exclamation of impatience.]

[Footnote 120: Milan. A public place.]

[Footnote 121: In escheat; here, in fee.]

[Footnote 122: Disbeliever.]

[Footnote 123: Fraught.]

[Footnote 124: A gallery in the residence of the Cardinal and Ferdinand.]

[Footnote 125: A dog which worries sheep.]

[Footnote 126: A fabulous serpent that killed by its glance.]

[Footnote 127: Cut a caper.]

[Footnote 128: Broth.]

[Footnote 129: Skeletons.]

[Footnote 130: So Dyce. Qq. BROUGHT.]

[Footnote 131: Perfumed sweetmeats for the breath.]

[Footnote 132: Smoke.]

[Footnote 133: A fortification.]

[Footnote 134: Milan. An apartment in the residence of the Cardinal and Ferdinand.]

[Footnote 135: Reality.]

[Footnote 136: Mistake.]

[Footnote 137: i.e., the dead body.]

[Footnote 138: Another apartment in the same.

www.ingramcontent.com/pod-product-compliance
Lightning Source LLC
Chambersburg PA
CBHW061444040426
42450CB00007B/1209